اے کاش حبیب

A Comprehensive Guide to

# Tajweed

Compiled by:

Muawiyah ibn (Mufti) Abdus-Samad

Teacher at Jamiatul Ilm Wal Huda

**Jamiatul Ilm Wal Huda**

All rights reserved. No part of this publication may be reproduced, stored in a retrieval system, or transmitted in any form by means of electronic, mechanical, photocopying or otherwise, without the prior permission of the distributors.

British Library Cataloguing in Publication Data

A catalogue record for this book is available from the British Library.

**Published & Distributed by**:

Jamiatul Ilm Wal Huda
30 Moss Street
Blackburn
Lancashire, U.K.
BB1 5JT
T: 01254 673105
W: www.jamiah.co.uk
E: info@jamiah.co.uk

**ISBN**: 978-0-9556973-3-3

**Printed by**: Imak Ofset, Turkey

بسم الله الرحمن الرحيم

In the Name of Allah, the Most Gracious, the Most Merciful

قال رسول الله ﷺ

"مَثَلُ الَّذِي يَقْرَأُ الْقُرْآنَ وَهُوَ حَافِظٌ لَهُ مَعَ السَّفَرَةِ الْكِرَامِ وَمَثَلُ الَّذِي يَقْرَأُ الْقُرْآنَ وَهُوَ يَتَعَاهَدُهُ وَهُوَ عَلَيْهِ شَدِيدٌ فَلَهُ أَجْرَانِ"

(متّفق عليه)

بسم الله الرحمن الرحيم

الحمد لله ربّ العالمين والصلاة والسلام على رحمة للعالمين ومن تبعه من النّاس أجمعين أمّا بعد

Reciting the Qur'an holds immense virtue, many Prophetic narrations and discourses of the guided scholars indicate upon the importance of Qura'nic recitation. However, all actions within Islam, an act is only regarded as rewarding if it is fulfilled according to the teachings of the Prophet *Muhammad* ﷺ. Likewise, reciting the Qur'an is only regarded an act of worship if it is performed in the Prophetic method; under the Prophetic guidance. The great 8th century scholar, Imam *Awza'ee* mentions:

"خَمْسٌ كَانَ عَلَيْهَا أَصْحَابُ مُحَمَّدٍ وَالتَّابِعُونَ بِإِحْسَانٍ: لُزُومُ الْجَمَاعَةِ وَاتِّبَاعُ السُّنَّةِ وَعِمَارَةُ الْمَسَاجِدِ وَتِلَاوَةُ الْقُرْآنِ وَالْجِهَادُ فِي سَبِيلِ اللَّهِ"[1]

'The companions of the Prophet and the followers were upon five attributes: [one] holding firm onto the (Muslim) congregation, [two] following the Sunnah, [three] building mosques [four] reading the Qur'an [five] fighting for the correct cause.'

Reciting the Qur'an is an act that is not only rewarding, instead a desire of every Muslim. The third caliph, *Uthman* (may Allah be pleased with him) mentions in a quote transmitted by *Ibn Rajab* in his book *'Jamiul uloomi wal hikm'* (1408AH):

"لَوْ طَهُرَتْ قُلُوبُكُمْ مَا شَبِعْتُمْ مِنْ كَلَامِ رَبِّكُمْ"

'If your hearts were clean, you will never be replete from the recitation of your lord's speech (the Qur'an)'.

Prophetic narrations are filled with the mentioning of the virtues for reciting the Qur'an; one virtue has been mentioned by Imam *Tirmidhi* in his famous Hadeeth compilation:

"اقْرَأْ وَارْتَقِ وَرَتِّلْ كَمَا كُنْتَ تُرَتِّلُ فِي الدُّنْيَا فَإِنَّ مَنْزِلَتَكَ عِنْدَ آخِرِ آيَةٍ تَقْرَأُ بِهَا"

'Recite and climb (the steps of paradise); recite how you recited in the world, your abode in paradise will be the place where you recite your last verse'.

Some scholars indicate that the method of reciting indicated in this Prophetic narration is 'perfecting the words (with pronunciation and qualities) and understanding the places of *waqf* (pausing)'[2].

---

[1] This quote is mentioned in *'nadhratun naeem'* (نضرة النعيم).

[2] This commentary has been indicated by *Muhammad Abdurrahman al-mubarakfuri* in his commentary upon the Imam *Tirmidhi* compilation.

We should indeed try to perfect our recitation, some deficiencies within the recitation can lead to changing the meaning of the Qur'an, other deficiencies may not lead to the changing of the Qur'an, and however, it would be disliked by many guided scholars. Therefore, the reciters of the Qur'an should realise that in reciting the 'speech of Allah – the Qur'an'; we should try our ultimate best to perfect our recitation.

Indeed understanding and learning the rules of *tajweed* is a definite help in perfecting the recitation; however, this subject is greatly dependent upon listening to the recitation from the guided tutors.

Further, it is very important to understand that reciting the Qur'an with the best of voices is not the only right of the Qur'an. Pondering upon the meaning of the Qur'an, lessons of the Qur'an, fulfilling its commandments and refraining from its prohibitions is the ultimate objective of serving the Qur'an according to its correct right. This is the commentary the great scholar of Hadeeth, *Abul Abbas al-Qurtubi* has given for the narration mentioned in the two authentic books of Hadeeth; *Saheehul Bukhari* and *Saheehul Muslim*. The narration is:

"يَقْرَؤُوْنَ الْقُرْآنَ لَا يُجَاوِزُ حَنَاجِرَهُمْ"

'[Some readers] read the Qur'an, yet the Qur'an does not pass their throats'.

In the commentary of this narration *Abul Abbas al-Qurtubi* mentions:

"يَسْتَطِيْبُوْنَ تِلَاوَتَهُ وَلَا يَفْهَمُوْنَ مَعَانِيْهِ"

'They [are those people] who decorate their recitation, however, do not understand the meaning'.

Another scholar, Ibn Abdil Barr al-Qurtubi mentions in its commentary:

"لَا يَنْتَفِعُوْنَ بِقِرَاءَتِهِ كَمَا لَا يَنْتَفِعُ الْآكِلُ وَالشَّارِبُ"

'[The narration is regarding those people] that do not benefit from what they recite, similar to a person who eats or drinks but does not take benefit from the sustenance [as it does not pass his throat]'.

Further, in the explanation of the narration 'the Qur'an can testify for you on the day of resurrection or against you'; the great scholar of Hadeeth, Imam *Nawawi* has mentioned,

"الْقُرْآنُ حُجَّةٌ لَكَ أَوْ عَلَيْكَ فَمَعْنَاهُ ظَاهِرٌ أَيْ تَنْتَفِعُ بِهِ إِنْ تَلَوْتَهُ وَعَمِلْتَ بِهِ وَإِلَّا فَهُوَ حُجَّةٌ عَلَيْكَ"

'… If you recite and act upon the Qur'an [then the Qur'an will intercede for you on the day of resurrection] or else it will testify against you'.

I make sincere dua to Almighty Allah that he enables us to perfect our recitation according to the method of the Prophet *Muhammad* ﷺ, and more importantly, work on acting upon the teachings of the Qur'an.

In completing this work, I firstly thank Almighty Allah upon the ability and the understanding he has given. Further, I thank all the people who have helped in compiling this book in terms of education; this includes my honourable father (Mufti) Abdus-Samad, teachers and beloved students of Jamiatul Ilm Wal Huda. Thanking is indeed a very important aspect of our religion as the wise have mentioned:

"مَنْ قَصُرَتْ يَدَاهُ عَنِ الْمُكَافَأَةِ فَلْيُطِلْ لِسَانَهُ بِالشُّكْرِ"

'Whosoever is unable to repay with his hands, he should thank in abundance with his tongue [making dua, etc]'.

Therefore, I thank all those who helped me complete this work. I finally ask Allah to place this small work and effort in our scale of good deeds, Verily He is the All-powerful and Supreme.

May Allah make the institute, Jamiatul Ilm Wal Huda (Blackburn, U.K.) and other institutes around the globe a means of guidance for mankind. Ameen.

**Muawiyah Ibn (Mufti) Abdus-Samad Ahmed**
**Graduate of Jamiatul Ilm Wal Huda (Blackburn, U.K.)**

# Table of Contents

Table of Contents ................................................................................. 7

Important terminologies ..................................................................... 12

Importance of *Tajweed* ....................................................................... 13

    Definition of *Tajweed*: ..................................................................... 13

    Subject of *Tajweed*: ......................................................................... 13

    Purpose of *Tajweed*: ........................................................................ 13

    Importance of praying with *Tajweed*: ............................................. 13

    Major & Minor mistakes: ................................................................ 13

الاستعاذة والبسملة ......................................................................................... 14

    استعاذة & its rules: ............................................................................ 14

    بسملة & its rules: ............................................................................. 15

Different methods of commencing Qura'nic recitation ...................... 16

    Methods of commencing Qura'nic recitation: ................................. 16

    Praying استعاذة & بسملة with another verse: .................................... 16

    Methods of praying استعاذة & بسملة with another verse: ................. 17

    Ruling of praying استعاذة & بسملة with a Qura'nic verse: ............... 18

The Teeth ............................................................................................. 19

The Tongue and its surroundings ........................................................ 20

Place of Pronunciation ......................................................................... 21

Diagram on the Place of Pronunciation .............................................. 23

Title of letters ....................................................................................... 24

Diagram on the Title of letters ............................................................. 25
Qualities of letters ............................................................................. 26
    Types of 'qualities' ........................................................................ 26
    Flowchart outlining the different qualities ................................. 27
Compulsory Qualities ....................................................................... 28
    Types of compulsory 'qualities': ................................................... 28
        The opposite 'qualities' .............................................................. 28
        The single 'qualities' .................................................................. 30
    The strong & weak qualities ......................................................... 32
Differences of the letters ................................................................... 35
Temporary Qualities .......................................................................... 37
    Brief explanation of the four 'Temporary qualities' ................... 38
    First type of 'temporary qualities – لازمة' ................................... 39
        Full mouth & empty mouth ..................................................... 40
        Levels of 'full mouth' recitation ................................................ 46
    Second type of 'temporary qualities – اتّصال' ............................. 47
        *Noon Saakin* and *Tanween* ...................................................... 48
        *Meem Saakin* ............................................................................ 58
        Rules of *Ghunnah* ..................................................................... 62
    Situations of two letters occurring next to each other ................ 63
        Letters occurring next to each other in terms of pronunciation & qualities ..................................................................................... 63

Letters occurring next to each other in terms of *Harakah* .................. 66

# Rules of the pronoun (ھ) ........................................................... 73

## Definition of the pronoun (ھ) ..................................................... 73

## Rules of the pronoun (ھ) ........................................................... 73

# Rules of the pronoun (ھ) and صلة ............................................... 74

## Definition of الصِّلَة ...................................................................... 74

## Rules of the pronoun (ھ) in terms of صلة .................................... 74

# Types & Rules of *Madd* ............................................................. 75

## Definition of *Madd* ................................................................... 75

### Letters of *Madd* ...................................................................... 75

### Types of *Madd* ....................................................................... 76

# *Waqf* .......................................................................................... 90

## Flowchart outlining the different discussions of *Waqf*: ............ 90

# *Waqf* .......................................................................................... 91

## Types of *Waqf* according to occurrence: ................................. 93

### Types of 'الوقف الاختياريّ': ....................................................... 95

## Types of *Waqf* according to pronunciation: ............................. 97

## Types of *Waqf* according to its original state ......................... 100

## Types of *Waqf* according to رسم and وصل ............................. 103

## Signs of *Waqf* and signs of *Wasl* ......................................... 105

## Types & Rules of *Sakt* ........................................................... 108

## Types & Rules of *Sukoot* ....................................................... 110

Types & Rules of *Qat'* ................................................................. 111

The three stages of recitation ............................................................ 112

*Hamzah* ............................................................................................ 113

    Types of *Hamzah* ......................................................................... 113

    Rules of *Hamzah* .......................................................................... 114

Method of reciting *Saakin* .................................................................. 117

Method of reciting the different *Harakaat* ........................................ 118

Method of reciting *Tashdeed* ............................................................. 119

*Imala'a* ............................................................................................. 120

Rules for *Tanween* .............................................................................. 121

    Definition of *Tanween* ................................................................. 121

    Rules for *Tanween* ....................................................................... 121

Meeting of two *Saakin's* ..................................................................... 122

    Rules for 'meeting of two *Saakin's*' ............................................. 123

Arabic Letters .................................................................................... 124

    Abjad order ................................................................................... 125

    Hija'i order .................................................................................... 126

Written transmission of the Qur'an .................................................. 127

Chapters of the Qur'an ...................................................................... 129

The Different Qira'ah ........................................................................ 133

Recitation according to *Hafs al-Asadi* ............................................... 136

    The letter (ص) or (س): ................................................................. 136

| | |
|---|---|
| Broken letters – حروف مقطّعات | 138 |
| Prostration Places within the Qur'an | 140 |
| Prophets mentioned in the Qur'an | 143 |
| Information regarding the Qur'an | 144 |
| Virtues regarding the Qur'an | 148 |
| Etiquettes of reading the Qur'an | 150 |
| Method of memorising the Qur'an | 152 |
| Chain of Qur'anic recitation | 153 |

# Important terminologies

Before discussing the detail rules regarding Qura'nic recitation, some important terminologies are mentioned.

|   | Sign | Explanation |
|---|------|-------------|
| 1 | َ | This is called a (single) *fathah*. |
| 2 | ُ | This is called a (single) *dhammah*. |
| 3 | ِ | This is called a (single) *kasrah*. |
| 4 | ْ | This is called a *saakin*. |
| 5 | ً | This is called a double *fathah*. |
| 6 | ٍ | This is called a double *kasrah*. |
| 7 | ٌ | This is called a double *dhammah*. |
| 8 | ّ | This is called a *tashdeed* and a letter with this upon it is called *mushaddad*. |
| 9 | Harakah | This is *fathah*, *dhammah* or *kasrah*. A letter which has a *harakah* upon it is called a *mutaharrik*. |
| 10 | Tanween | This is 'double *fathah*', 'double *dhammah*' or a 'double *kasrah*'. |
| 11 | حرف (حروف) | This is the Arabic word for 'letter'. |
| 12 | مخرج (مخارج) | This is the Arabic word for 'places of pronunciation'. |
| 13 | صفة (صفات) | This is the Arabic word for 'qualities'. |
| 14 | لقب (ألقاب) | This is the Arabic word for 'titles' (the different titles given to the different letters). |
| 15 | مضاعف | This is the name given to 'letters occurring twice (together)'. |
| 16 | الحروف المقطّعات | This is the name given to the beginning letters of certain chapters of the Qur'an like الم. |
| 17 | الحروف القمرية | This is the name given to the letters which are pronounced without a *tashdeed* when (ال) is placed before it. |
| 18 | الحروف الشمسيّة | This is the name given to the letters which are pronounced with a *tashdeed* when (ال) is placed before it. |

# Importance of *Tajweed*

## Definition of *Tajweed*:

To pray all the letters from the **correct 'place of pronunciation'** and with the **correct 'qualities'**.

## Subject of *Tajweed*:

Tajweed discusses the individual letters of the alphabet; in terms of their 'place of pronunciation' and 'qualities'.

## Purpose of *Tajweed*:

To correct the pronunciation and gain maximum reward by making the pronunciation as close to the Prophet ﷺ as possible.

## Importance of praying with *Tajweed*:

If a person changes the word by **addition, deletion or substitution of a letter** (or certain *harakaat*), which results in the changing of the meaning of the word; this person will be **deemed sinful**.

If the reciter changes the **'qualities'** (or certain *harakaat*) he will be **worthy of punishment**.

## Major & Minor mistakes:

|   | Type of mistake | Definition | Ruling |
|---|---|---|---|
| 1 | **Major mistakes** <br> This is called اللحن الجليّ | Changing the word by **addition, deletion or substitution of a letter** (or certain *harakaat*). | This type of recitation is *haram*; hence, the reciter is sinful if these mistakes are made on purpose. |
| 2 | **Minor mistakes** <br> This is called اللحن الخفيّ | Changing the **'qualities'** of a letter (or certain *harakaat*). | This type of recitation is *makrooh*; in these mistakes the reciter should fear punishment. |

**Note**: If a person recitation is not upto the correct standard, the individual should continue to strive in improving his/her recitation by a learned scholar. However, he/she should not despair in his/her recitation as there are Prophetic narrations which indicate upon double reward for a person who finds it hard to recite but continues to recite whilst striving for improvement.

الاستعاذة والبسملة

## استعاذة & its rules:

**What is استعاذة ?** It is the recitation of أعوذ بالله من الشيطان الرجيم when commencing the Qura'nic recitation.

**What is the ruling of استعاذة ?**

It is **important** to pray استعاذة before you start praying the Qur'an; according to **some scholars** it is **compulsory**. Most scholars mention it is preferable to pray استعاذة before starting the recitation.

Also, if inbetween your recitation you say something other than the recitation of the Qur'an, you **should** pray استعاذة again. Certain scholars add that taking a long pause for rest, etc, during the recitation will also make it **preferable** to pray استعاذة again.

<u>Note</u>: Some scholars have mentioned that استعاذة is prayed after the completion of recitation; **however, this is a weak view**.

**Should استعاذة be prayed loudly or quietly?**

Generally, the volume of recitation for استعاذة corresponds to the volume of the Qura'nic recitation. If the Qura'nic recitation is loud then استعاذة will be prayed loudly, **except in certain circumstances like Salaah**. If the Qura'nic recitation is quiet then استعاذة will be prayed quietly.

**Which words can be used for استعاذة ?**

Any sentence can be used which indicates upon seeking refuge from the devil, however the best form is to pray:

أَعُوْذُ بِاللهِ مِنَ الشَّيْطَانِ الرَّجِيْمِ

Other forms include:

(1) أَعُوْذُ بِاللهِ السَّمِيْعِ الْعَلِيْمِ مِنَ الشَّيْطَانِ الرَّجِيْمِ

(2) اللَّهُمَّ إِنِّي أَعُوْذُ بِكَ مِنْ إِبْلِيْسَ وَجُنُوْدِهِ

(3) أَعُوْذُ بِاللهِ مِنَ الشَّيْطَانِ

# بسملة & its rules:

**What is بسملة ?** It is the recitation of بسم الله الرحمن الرحيم when commencing the Qura'nic recitation, after the recitation of استعاذة.

## What is the ruling of بسملة ?

It is **important** to pray بسم الله الرحمن الرحيم at the beginning of ALL the chapters of the Qur'an **except** at the beginning of سورة البراءة (9th chapter of the Qur'an).

However, if a person's recitation begins from **inbetween** a chapter then it is **optional but preferable** to pray بسملة. This includes beginning the recitation from inbetween سورة البراءة.

## How will استعاذة and بسملة be prayed?

According to some scholars it is better to separate the two, therefore after استعاذة have a pause and then pray بسملة. Other scholars say any method can be chosen; both are equally valid.

# Different methods of commencing Qura'nic recitation

## Methods of commencing Qura'nic recitation:
*(handwritten note: scenarios)*

There are two methods to start the recitation of the Qur'an:
1. ابْتِدَاءُ الْقِرَاءَةِ وَابْتِدَاءُ السُّورَةِ – starting the recitation from the **beginning** of a chapter.
2. ابْتِدَاءُ الْقِرَاءَةِ وَوَسَطُ السُّورَةِ – starting the recitation from the **middle** of a chapter.

Example of starting the recitation from the **beginning** of a chapter:

أَعُوذُ بِاللهِ مِنَ الشَّيْطَانِ الرَّجِيمِ ﴿1﴾ بِسْمِ اللهِ الرَّحْمٰنِ الرَّحِيمِ ﴿2﴾ قُلْ هُوَ اللهُ أَحَدٌ ﴿3﴾

Example of starting the recitation from the **middle** of a chapter:

أَعُوذُ بِاللهِ مِنَ الشَّيْطَانِ الرَّجِيمِ ﴿1﴾ بِسْمِ اللهِ الرَّحْمٰنِ الرَّحِيمِ ﴿2﴾ مَالِكِ يَوْمِ الدِّينِ ﴿3﴾

## Praying بسملة & استعاذة with another verse:

There are **three** different situations possible for a reciter when praying استعاذة and بسملة with another Qura'nic verse.

1. The reciter is **starting the recitation** from the **beginning** of a chapter.
   This is called ابْتِدَاءُ الْقِرَاءَةِ وَابْتِدَاءُ السُّورَةِ.

**Example**:

أَعُوذُ بِاللهِ مِنَ الشَّيْطَانِ الرَّجِيمِ ﴿1﴾ بِسْمِ اللهِ الرَّحْمٰنِ الرَّحِيمِ ﴿2﴾ قُلْ هُوَ اللهُ أَحَدٌ ﴿3﴾

2. The reciter is **starting the recitation** from the **middle** of a chapter.
   This is called ابْتِدَاءُ الْقِرَاءَةِ وَوَسَطُ السُّورَةِ.

**Example**:

أَعُوذُ بِاللهِ مِنَ الشَّيْطَانِ الرَّجِيمِ ﴿1﴾ بِسْمِ اللهِ الرَّحْمٰنِ الرَّحِيمِ ﴿2﴾ مَالِكِ يَوْمِ الدِّينِ ﴿3﴾

3. The reciter is **continuing the recitation** (finishing one chapter and starting the next chapter). This is called وَسَطُ الْقِرَاءَةِ وَابْتِدَاءُ السُّورَةِ.

**Example**:

وَمِنْ شَرِّ حَاسِدٍ إِذَا حَسَدَ ﴿1﴾ بِسْمِ اللهِ الرَّحْمٰنِ الرَّحِيمِ ﴿2﴾ قُلْ أَعُوذُ بِرَبِّ النَّاسِ ﴿3﴾

# Methods of praying بسملة & استعاذة with another verse:

Each of the **three** situations mentioned above for praying بسملة & استعاذة with another Qura'nic verse can be read in **four possible methods**. However, one of these possible methods is **forbidden**.

The table below shows the **four possible methods**:

| | Method | Explanation |
|---|---|---|
| 1 | فَصْلُ الْكُلّ | **Separating all 3 parts from each other.** <br> Separating استعاذة from بسملة and separating بسملة from the Qura'nic verse. |
| 2 | وَصْلُ الْكُلّ | **Joining all 3 parts with each other.** <br> Joining استعاذة with بسملة and joining بسملة with the Qura'nic verse. |
| 3 | فَصْلُ الْأَوَّل وَوَصْلُ الثَّانِي | **Separating the first two and joining the second and third.** <br> Separating استعاذة from بسملة , however joining بسملة with the Qura'nic verse. |
| 4 | وَصْلُ الْأَوَّل وَفَصْلُ الثَّانِي | **Joining the first two and separating the second and third.** <br> Joining استعاذة with بسملة , however separating بسملة with the Qura'nic verse. |

<u>Note</u>: When **separating** the different parts, it is important to note that a **pause** is done with a normal breath and **not a long delay**. Also, when **joining** there should be no breath taken.

The table below shows examples for the **four possible methods**:

| | Method | Example |
|---|---|---|
| 1 | فَصْلُ الْكُلّ | أَعُوْذُ بِاللهِ مِنَ الشَّيْطَانِ الرَّجِيْمِ ﴿pause﴾ بِسْمِ اللهِ الرَّحْمٰنِ الرَّحِيْمِ ﴿pause﴾ قُلْ هُوَ اللهُ أَحَدٌ |
| 2 | وَصْلُ الْكُلّ | أَعُوْذُ بِاللهِ مِنَ الشَّيْطَانِ الرَّجِيْمِ ﴿join﴾ بِسْمِ اللهِ الرَّحْمٰنِ الرَّحِيْمِ ﴿join﴾ قُلْ هُوَ اللهُ أَحَدٌ |
| 3 | فَصْلُ الْأَوَّل وَوَصْلُ الثَّانِي | أَعُوْذُ بِاللهِ مِنَ الشَّيْطَانِ الرَّجِيْمِ ﴿pause﴾ بِسْمِ اللهِ الرَّحْمٰنِ الرَّحِيْمِ ﴿join﴾ قُلْ هُوَ اللهُ أَحَدٌ |
| 4 | وَصْلُ الْأَوَّل وَفَصْلُ الثَّانِي | أَعُوْذُ بِاللهِ مِنَ الشَّيْطَانِ الرَّجِيْمِ ﴿join﴾ بِسْمِ اللهِ الرَّحْمٰنِ الرَّحِيْمِ ﴿pause﴾ قُلْ هُوَ اللهُ أَحَدٌ |

# Ruling of praying بسملة & استعاذة with a Qura'nic verse:

We have learnt there are 3 possible situations with 4 possible methods of praying استعاذة & بسملة with a Qura'nic verse.

The table below mentions the rulings for reciting استعاذة & بسملة with a Qura'nic verse in the different situations with the different methods:

|   | Method | ابتداء القراءة وابتداء السورة | ابتداء القراءة ووسط السورة | وسط القراءة وابتداء السورة |
|---|---|---|---|---|
| 1 | فَصْلُ الكُلّ (see عليهم) | Permissible | Permissible | Permissible |
| 2 | وَصْلُ الكُلّ (good) | Permissible | Not good (as) | Not good (as) |
| 3 | فَصْلُ الأَوَّل وَوَصْلُ الثَّاني | Permissible (Not good) | Not good (as) | Permissible |
| 4 | وَصْلُ الأَوَّل وفَصْلُ الثَّاني | Permissible | Permissible | Not permissible |

**Brief**: From amongst the different situations it is important to note that when **starting** the recitation from the **middle** of a chapter, it is **preferable** to pray the Qura'nic verse **separately** (after a pause). Also, when **continuing** the recitation from one chapter to another, it is **preferable** (and in one case **compulsory**) to pray the last verse of the last chapter **separately**, i.e. praying the **last verse** and then pausing before reciting بسملة.

**Note**: It is also permissible to do سكت between استعاذة, بسملة and the following verse. The rules of سكت are discussed later; in the chapter of *Waqf*.

# The Teeth

Before discussing the pronunciation and 'qualities' of the different letters, it is helpful to know the names given to the different teeth in Arabic.

The following diagram illustrates the teeth with their names.

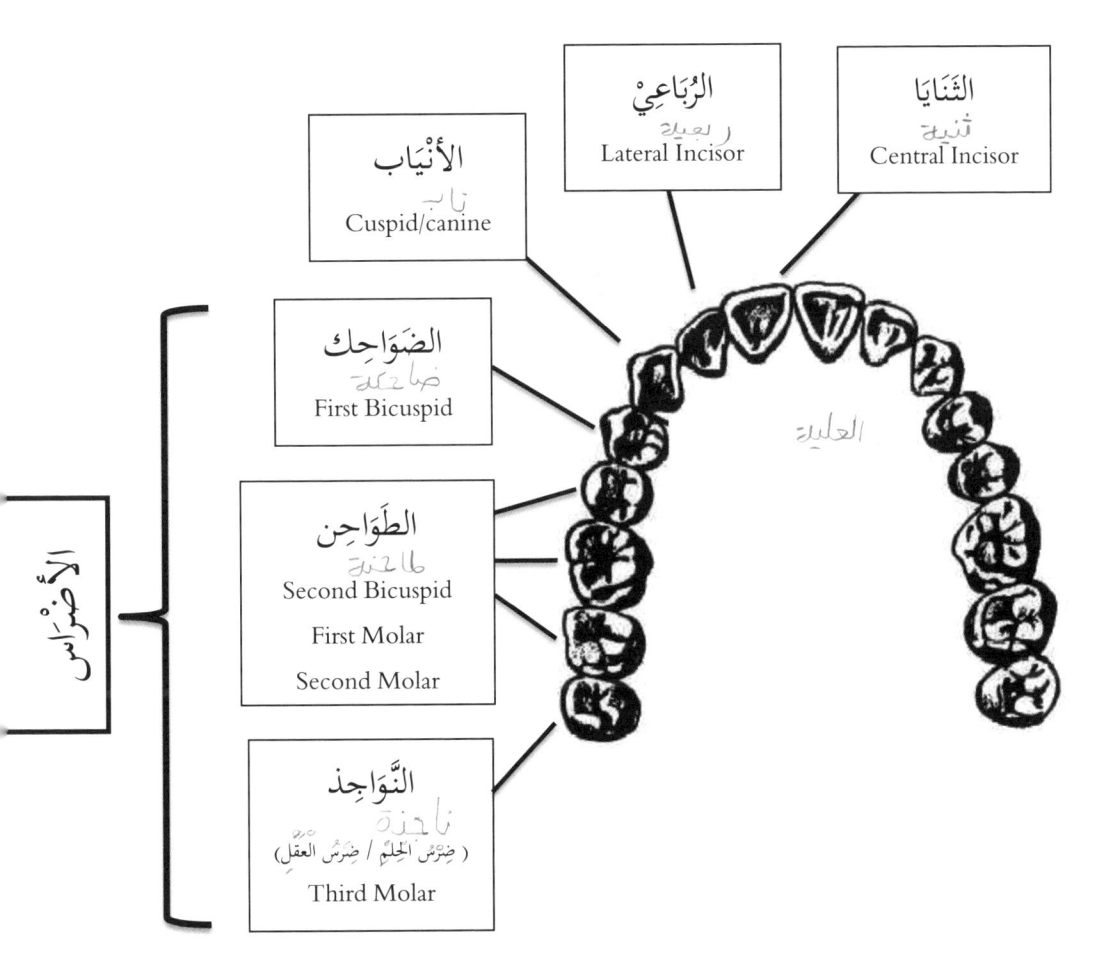

**الثَّنَايَا**
Central Incisor

**الرُّبَاعِي**
Lateral Incisor

**الأَنْيَاب**
Cuspid/canine

**الضَّوَاحِك**
First Bicuspid

**الطَّوَاحِن**
Second Bicuspid
First Molar
Second Molar

**النَّوَاجِذ**
(ضِرْسُ الحِلْمِ / ضِرْسُ العَقْلِ)
Third Molar

**Note**:

The diagram only shows the top teeth, the bottom teeth have the same names. Also, only 8 teeth are labelled, the opposite teeth will have the same names. In total their will be 32 teeth, 16 at the top and 16 at the bottom.

**The top teeth are called** العُلْيَا **in Arabic and the bottom teeth are called** السُّفْلَى . **Also, the Bicuspids and molars are called** الأَضْرَاس **in Arabic**.

19

# The Tongue and its surroundings

Before discussing the pronunciation and 'qualities' of the different letters, it is helpful to know the names given to the different areas of the tongue and its surroundings in Arabic.

The following diagram illustrates the different areas of the tongue and its surroundings with its names.

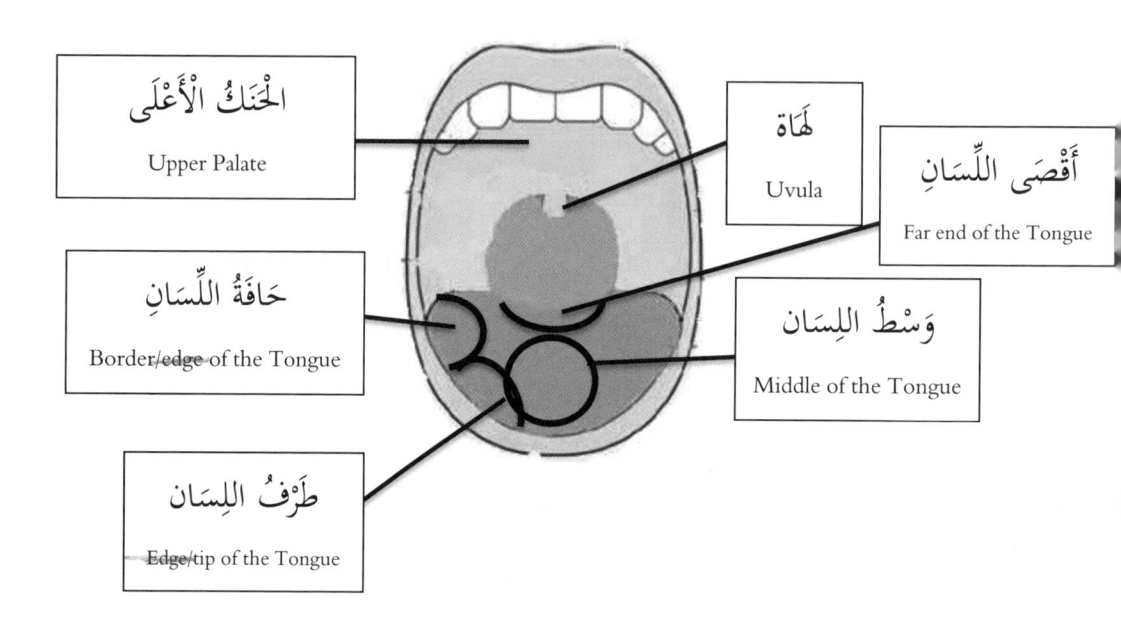

الْحَنَكُ الْأَعْلَى
Upper Palate

لَهَاة
Uvula

أَقْصَى اللِّسَانِ
Far end of the Tongue

حَافَةُ اللِّسَانِ
Border/edge of the Tongue

وَسْطُ اللِسَان
Middle of the Tongue

طَرَفُ اللِسَانِ
Edge/tip of the Tongue

**Other terms**:

| | Part (Arabic name) | Part (English name) |
|---|---|---|
| 1 | لِثَّة | Gum(s) |
| 2 | شَفَة | Lip(s) |
| 3 | لِسَان | Tongue |
| 4 | أَدْنَى الْحَلْق | The top part of the throat (close to the mouth) |
| 5 | وَسْطُ الْحَلْق | The middle part of the throat |
| 6 | أَقْصَى الْحَلْق | The bottom part of the throat (close to the chest) |

# Place of Pronunciation

Every letter from amongst the 29 different letters in Arabic have their individual place of pronunciation. In total the different places of pronunciation can be categorised into 17 places. The 'place of pronunciation' is called the مخرج (plural مخارج) of the letter.

The following table mentions all the letters with their 'place of pronunciation':

|   | Letter | Place of Pronunciation |
|---|--------|------------------------|
| 1 | الحروف المدّة<br>( َ ا ، ُ و ، ِ ي ) | Empty space within the mouth. |
| 2 | ء ، هـ | Far end of the throat (end close to the chest). |
| 3 | ع ، ح | Middle part of the throat. |
| 4 | غ ، خ | Near end of the throat (end close to the mouth). |
| 5 | ق | Far end of the tongue (end close to the throat) **joint** with the upper palate of the mouth. |
| 6 | ك | Far end of the tongue (end close to the throat) **joint** with the upper palate of the mouth, but slightly further away **from** the throat than the letter (ق). |
| 7 | ج ، ش ،<br>الياء غير المديّة | Middle part of the tongue **joint** with the upper palate of the mouth. |
| 8 | ض | One of the edges of the tongue (the far edge, the edge close to the throat) **joint** with the top molars. |

| | | |
|---|---|---|
| 9 | ل | The edge of the tongue (slightly closer to the front of the mouth than the edge used for (ض)) **joint** with the gums. |
| 10 | ن | The edge of the tongue (slightly closer to the front of the mouth than the edge used for (ل)) **joint** with the gums. |
| 11 | ر | The edge of the tongue (slightly closer to the front of the mouth than the edge used for (ن)) and the bottom side of the tongue **joint** with the gums. |
| 12 | ط ، د ، ت | The edge of the tongue (very close to the tip of the tongue) with the **roots** of the top front two teeth. |
| 13 | ظ ، ذ ، ث | The edge of the tongue (very close to the tip of the tongue) with the **tip** of the top front two teeth. |
| 14 | ص ، س ، ز | The edge of the tongue (very close to the tip of the tongue) with the **tip** of the bottom front two teeth and the **tip** of the front two teeth. |
| 15 | ف | The (inner) bottom lip and the **tip** of the top front two teeth. |
| 16 | ب ، م ، الواو غير المدّيّة | The two lips together. |
| 17 | ن ، م (في حالة إخفائهما أو إدغامهما) (in the state of *ikhfaa* or *idghaam*)* | The far end of the nose. |

\* These chapters will be discussed later.

**Note**: Some scholars have mentioned 17 different 'places of pronunciation' as mentioned above. Some scholars have only mentioned 16 'places of pronunciation'; they ignore the 1st 'place of pronunciation' mentioned, placing *alif* in the 2nd, *waaw* in the 16th and *yaa* in the 7th 'place of pronunciation'. Other scholars have only mentioned 14 'places of pronunciation'; they ignore the 1st 'place of pronunciation'; further they merge the 9th, 10th and 11th into one; hence in total 14 will be left.

# Diagram on the Place of Pronunciation

The following diagram visually indicates the 'place of pronunciation' for the different letters.

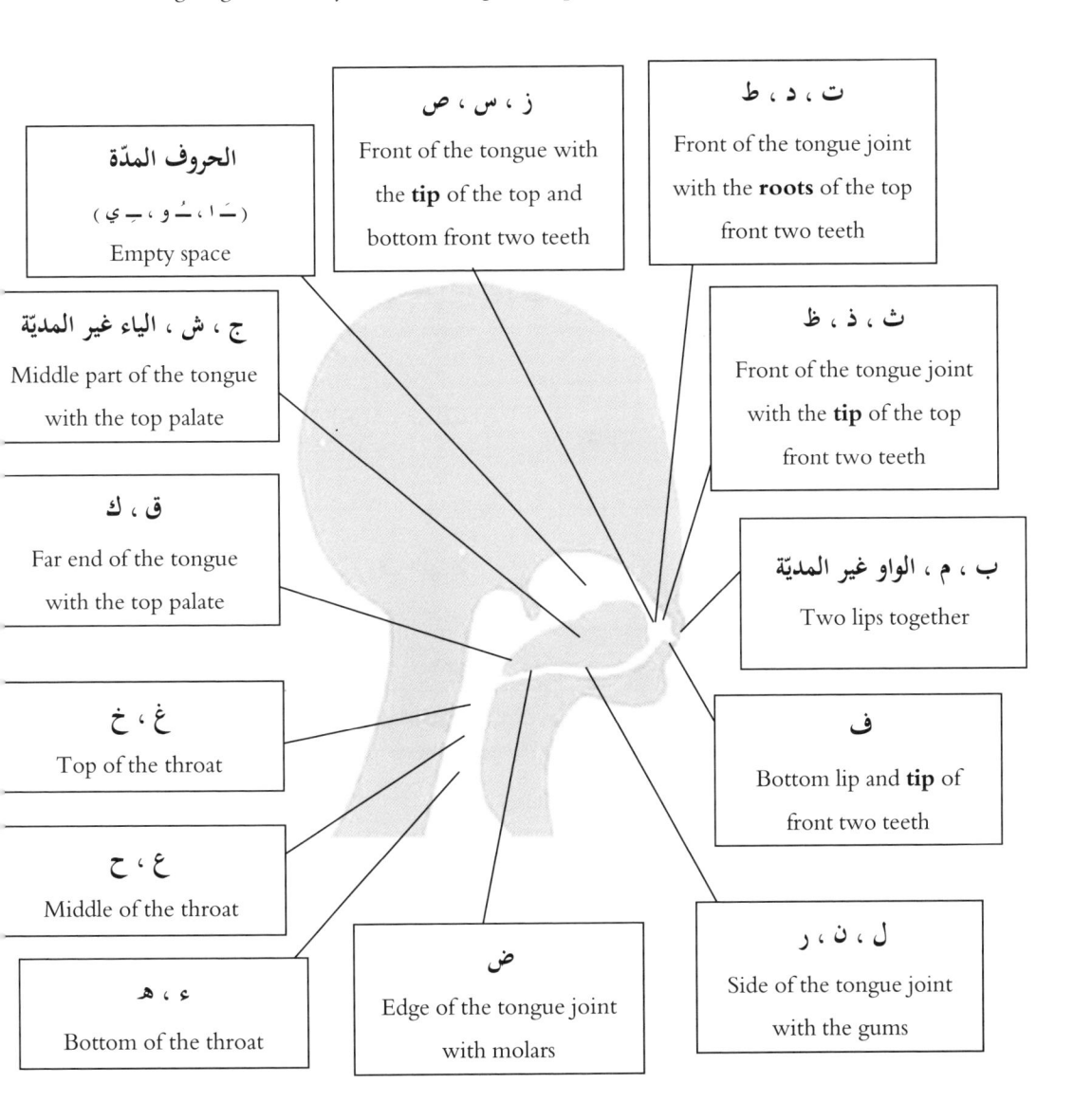

**ز ، س ، ص**
Front of the tongue with the **tip** of the top and bottom front two teeth

**ت ، د ، ط**
Front of the tongue joint with the **roots** of the top front two teeth

**الحروف المدّة**
( َـ ا ، ُـ و ، ِـ ي )
Empty space

**ج ، ش ، الياء غير المديّة**
Middle part of the tongue with the top palate

**ث ، ذ ، ظ**
Front of the tongue joint with the **tip** of the top front two teeth

**ق ، ك**
Far end of the tongue with the top palate

**ب ، م ، الواو غير المديّة**
Two lips together

**غ ، خ**
Top of the throat

**ف**
Bottom lip and **tip** of front two teeth

**ع ، ح**
Middle of the throat

**ء ، هـ**
Bottom of the throat

**ض**
Edge of the tongue joint with molars

**ل ، ن ، ر**
Side of the tongue joint with the gums

23

# Title of letters

Every letter from amongst the 29 different letters in Arabic have their individual title, the titles are based on their 'place of pronunciation'.

The title of the letter is called the لقب (plural ألقاب).

The following table mentions all the letters with their titles:

| | Letter | Title of letters |
|---|---|---|
| 1 | الحروف المدّة ( ـَـ ا ، ـُـ و ، ـِـ ي ) | الْحُرُوفُ الْجَوْفِيَّة (الحروف الهَوَائِيَّة) |
| 2 | ء ، هـ | الحروف الْحَلْقِيَّة |
| 3 | ع ، ح | |
| 4 | غ ، خ | |
| 5 | ق | الحروف اللَّهَوِيَّة |
| 6 | ك | |
| 7 | ج ، ش ، الياء غير المديّة | الحروف الشَّجَرِيَّة |
| 8 | ض | الحرفُ الْحَافِيَّة |
| 9 | ل | الحروف الطَّرَفِيَّة (الحروف الذلْقِيَّة) |
| 10 | ن | |
| 11 | ر | |
| 12 | ت ، د ، ط | الحروف النِّطْعِيَّة |
| 13 | ث ، ذ ، ظ | الحروف اللِّثَوِيَّة |
| 14 | ز ، س ، ص | الحروف الأَسَلِيَّة |
| 15 | ف | الحروف الشَّفَوِيَّة |
| 16 | ب ، م ، الواو غير المديّة | |

# Diagram on the Title of letters

The following diagram visually indicates the 'title of letters' for the different letters.

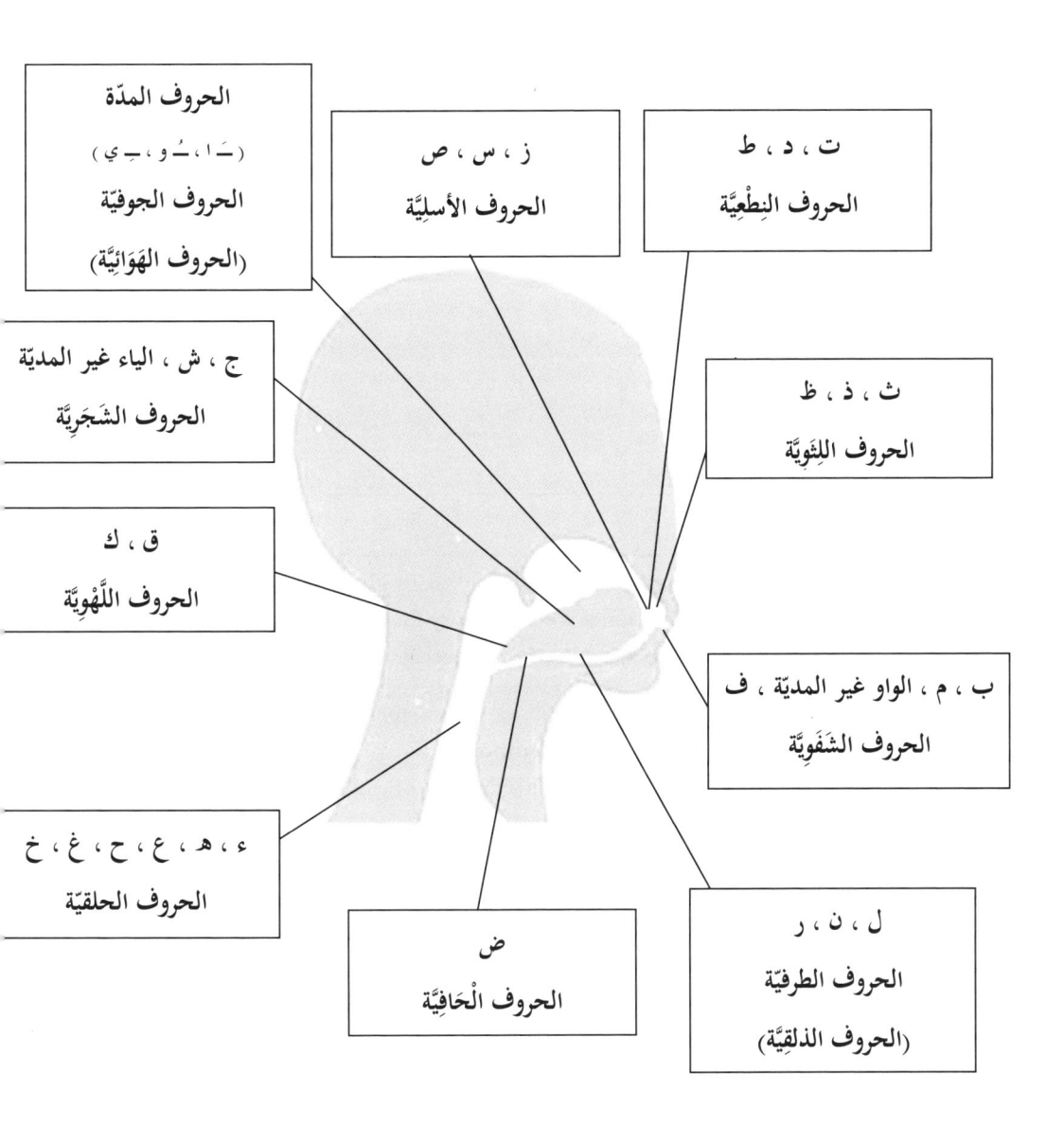

| | | |
|---|---|---|
| الحروف المدّة<br>(ـَـا ، ـُـو ، ـِـي)<br>الحروف الجوفيّة<br>(الحروف الهَوَائيّة) | ز ، س ، ص<br>الحروف الأسليّة | ت ، د ، ط<br>الحروف النِطْعِيّة |
| ج ، ش ، الياء غير المديّة<br>الحروف الشَجَريّة | | ث ، ذ ، ظ<br>الحروف اللِثَويّة |
| ق ، ك<br>الحروف اللَّهَويّة | | ب ، م ، الواو غير المديّة ، ف<br>الحروف الشَفَويّة |
| ء ، هـ ، ع ، ح ، غ ، خ<br>الحروف الحلقيّة | ض<br>الحروف الْحَافِيَّة | ل ، ن ، ر<br>الحروف الطرفيّة<br>(الحروف الذلقيّة) |

# Qualities of letters

Every letter from amongst the 29 different letters in Arabic have different 'qualities' by which the individual letter is pronounced. Each letter will have atleast five 'qualities', the "place of pronunciation" coupled with the "qualities" of each letter' will distinguish all the 29 different letters.

The quality of the letter is called the صفة (plural صفات).

## Types of 'qualities'

There are two types of صفات :

- (الصفات اللازمة compulsory 'qualities')
- (الصفات العارضة temporary 'qualities')

The following table defines each type:

|   | Type | Definition |
|---|---|---|
| 1 | الصفات اللازمة | These are such 'qualities' that are **always present** in the letter it appears with, it is **compulsory** for the letter to have these 'qualities' irrespective of what precedes the letter or what follows. |
| 2 | الصفات العارضة | These are such 'qualities' that are **not always present** in the letter it appears with, it is **temporary** for the letter to have these 'qualities' depending on what comes before, after the letter, etc. |

Both the types mentioned have further types; these will be discussed within the relevant chapters. Below is a flowchart which outlines the types.

Thereafter, 'compulsory qualities' will be discussed and then the 'temporary qualities'.

# Flowchart outlining the different qualities

The following flowchart outlines the chapters of 'qualities' – compulsory & temporary 'qualities' which are discussed in the following pages:

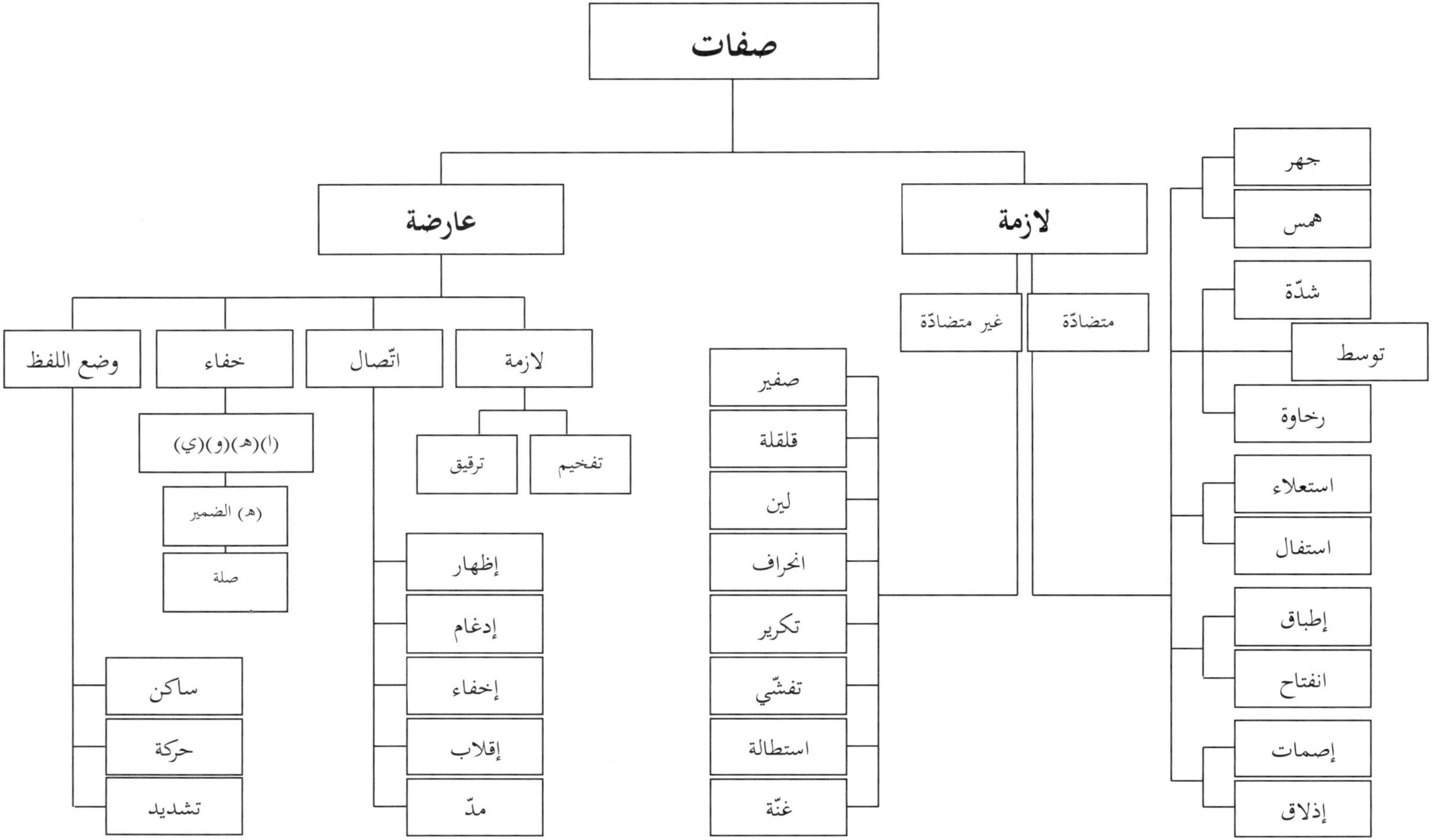

# Compulsory Qualities

## Types of compulsory 'qualities':

There are two types of compulsory 'qualities':

- الصفات المتضادّة ('opposite qualities')
- الصفات غير المتضادّة ('single qualities')

The following table defines each type:

|   | Type | Definition |
|---|---|---|
| 1 | الصفات المتضادّة | These are such 'qualities' which have 'opposite qualities'. Some letters have a certain 'quality' and the remaining letters **have** the 'opposite quality'. |
| 2 | الصفات غير المتضادّة | These are such 'qualities' which don't have 'opposite qualities'. Some letters have a certain 'quality', however this does **not** mean the remaining letters will have an 'opposite quality'. |

## The opposite 'qualities'

In total there are ten 'opposite qualities', five **pairs**. These are mentioned below:

| | Pair | |
|---|---|---|
| | **Strong** | **Weak** |
| 1 | الجهر | الهمس |
| 2 | الشدّة | الرخاوة |
| 3 | الاستعلاء | الاستفال |
| 4 | الإطباق | الانفتاح |
| 5 | الإصمات | الإذلاق |

**Note**: Not all the letters are covered in the second pair ( الشدّة – الرخاوة ). There are some letters which are neither from the letters of الشدّة nor from the letters of رخاوة. Instead, they are from an inbetween type which is called التوسّط. Therefore, in total there are 11 types.

The following table defines each 'opposite quality' with the letters they represent:

| | Quality | Definition | Letters | |
|---|---|---|---|---|
| 1 | الجهر | **Dictionary**: 'to raise'<br>**Terminology**: The voice is 'raised' to such an extent that when reciting the letter breathing stops. | ظَلَّ قُوُّرٍ بِضٍّ إِذْ غَزَا جُنْدٌ مُطِيعٌ | 19 |
| 2 | الهمس | **Dictionary**: 'to lower'<br>**Terminology**: The voice is 'lowered' to such an extent that when reciting the letter breathing continues. | فَحَثَّهُ شَخْصٌ سَكَتَ | 10 |
| 3 | الشدّة | **Dictionary**: 'to be strong'<br>**Terminology**: The voice is so 'strong' that when reciting the letter the voice stops straight away. | أَجِدُ قَطٍّ بَكَتْ | 8 |
| 4 | الرخاوة | **Dictionary**: 'to be soft'.<br>**Terminology**: The voice is so 'soft' that when reciting the letter the voice continues. | شَخْصٌ سَاحِفٌ هَوَّزٍ ثَيَّدَ ضَظَّغْ | 16 |
| 5 | التوسط | **Dictionary**: 'to be inbetween'<br>**Terminology**: The voice is not 'powerful' and nor is it 'soft', instead it is inbetween. Hence, the voice doesn't stop straight away and nor does it continue for long, instead the voice continues for a **short** while. | لِنْ عُمَرَ | 5 |
| 6 | الاستعلاء | **Dictionary**: 'to be raised'<br>**Terminology**: The tongue is 'raised', touching the upper palate of the mouth whilst reciting the letter. | خُصَّ ضَغْطٍ قِظْ | 7 |
| 7 | الاستفال | **Dictionary**: 'to be lowered'<br>**Terminology**: The tongue is 'lowered', not touching the upper palate of the mouth whilst reciting the letter. | ثَبَتَ عِزُّ مَنْ يُجَوِّدُ حَرْفَهُ إِذْ سَلَّ شَكَا | 22 |
| 8 | الإطباق | **Dictionary**: 'to close'<br>**Terminology**: The tongue is so close to the upper palate of the mouth that it completely 'closes' the upper palate whilst reciting the letter. | ص ، ض ، ط ، ظ | 4 |
| 9 | الانفتاح | **Dictionary**: 'to be open'<br>**Terminology**: The tongue isn't so close to the upper palate of the mouth that it completely 'closes' the upper palate. Instead, it's 'open' for air to pass whilst reciting. | مَنْ أَخَذَ وَجَدَ سَعَةً فَزَكَا حَقٌّ لَهُ شُرْبُ غَيْثٍ | 25 |
| 10 | الإصمات | **Dictionary**: 'to make stop'<br>**Terminology**: The words are pronounced firmly by 'stopping' the tongue at its 'place of pronunciation'. | جَزْ غَشَّ سَاخِطٍ صَدْ ثِقَةٍ إِذْ وَعَظَهُ يَحُضُّكَ | 23 |
| 11 | الإذلاق | **Dictionary**: 'to make slip'<br>**Terminology**: The words are pronounced quickly by 'slipping' the tongue from its 'place of pronunciation'. | فَرَّ مِنْ لُبٍّ | 6 |

# The single 'qualities'

In total there are eight 'single qualities'.

The following table defines each 'single quality' with the letters they represent:

| | Quality | Definition | Letters | |
|---|---|---|---|---|
| 1 | الصفير | **Dictionary**: 'to whistle'.<br>**Terminology**: It is a 'quality' in which a 'whistling' noise is created between lips when pronouncing the letter. | ز ، س ، ص | 3 |
| 2 | القلقلة | **Dictionary**: 'to shake'<br>**Terminology**: It is a 'quality' in which a 'shaking' noise is created when pronouncing the letter with a *saakin*. | قُطْبُ جَدٍّ | 5 |
| 3 | اللين | **Dictionary**: 'to be soft'<br>**Terminology**: It is a 'quality' in which the letters are pronounced with a 'soft' noise. | (و) *saakin* with a *fathah* before it.<br>**Example** (خَوْف)<br>(ي) *saakin* with a *fathah* before it.<br>**Example** (بَيْت) | 2 |
| 4 | الانحراف | **Dictionary**: 'to deviate'<br>**Terminology**: It is a 'quality' in which the letters, once pronounced from their own مخرج , 'deviate' into another مخرج. | ل ، ر | 2 |
| 5 | التكرير | **Dictionary**: 'to repeat'<br>**Terminology**: It is a 'quality' in which the tip of the tongue 'shakes' (repeats) when pronouncing the letter. | ر | 1 |
| 6 | التفشّي | **Dictionary**: 'to spread'<br>**Terminology**: It is a 'quality' in which the air and noise 'spreads' across the mouth when reciting the letter. | ش | 1 |
| 7 | الاستطالة | **Dictionary**: 'to spread'<br>**Terminology**: It is a 'quality' in which the voice 'spreads' through the edge of the tongue. | ض | 1 |
| 8 | الغنّة | **Dictionary**: 'nasal snuffle'<br>**Terminology**: It is a 'quality' in which the noise along with the mouth is produced in the nose. | ن ، م | 2 |

**Notes**:

(1) Out of the 5 letters of قلقلة, the letter (ق) has the strongest 'quality' of *qalqalah*. The *qalqalah* of the letter (ق) is **compulsory**, and in the remaining 4 letters it is **preferable**.

(2) The 'quality' of *qalqalah* has 3 different levels depending on the state of the *saakin* upon the letter. The table below defines and explains with examples.

|   | *Saakin* type | Example | Explanation |
|---|---|---|---|
| 1 | الْمُشَدَّد الْمَوْقُوْف عَلَيْه<br>Stopping on a letter which has a *tashdeed*. | الْحَقُّ | If you stop on this word then there will be a very strong *qalqalah* as it is a word which originally has a *tashdeed*. |
| 2 | غَيْرُ الْمُشَدَّد الْمَوْقُوْف عَلَيْه<br>Stopping on a letter which does not have a *tashdeed*, it has a *harakah*. | خَلَقَ | If you stop on this word then there will be an intermediate *qalqalah* as it is a word which originally has no *tashdeed*. |
| 3 | السَّاكِنُ وَصْلًا<br>*Qalqalah* on a letter which has an original *saakin*. | اقْرَأْ | If you stop on this word then there will be little *qalqalah* as it is a word which originally has a *saakin*. |

(3) The 'quality' of تكرير is mentioned above. The reason for mentioning this 'quality' is to make the reciter refrain from this 'quality', **NOT** bring this 'quality' into practice. The reader should limit the shaking caused by reciting the letter (ر), the shaking should **not** stop completely. Some scholars have mentioned تكرير (slight shaking) to be necessary, however, تكرار (intense shaking) to be forbidden.

# The strong & weak qualities

There were two categories of الصفات mentioned previously:

- الصفات المتضادّة (opposite 'qualities')
- الصفات غير المتضادّة (single 'qualities')

All the الصفات غير المتضادّة are referred to as الصفات القويّة (strong 'qualities') **except** for اللين.

However, from the الصفات المتضادّة only five are regarded as الصفات القويّة (strong 'qualities'). They are:

(1) الجهر (2) الشدّة (3) الاستعلاء (4) الإطباق (5) الإصمات

The remaining الصفات المتضادّة are regarded as الصفات الضعيفة (weak 'qualities'), **except** المتوسّط is regarded inbetween; not strong or weak.

The strength of the word and its weakness is dependent upon the amount of strong or weak 'qualities' it possesses.

The following table mentions the 'qualities' and analyses the strength of each letter:

|    | Letter | Qualities | Strong | Weak | Result |
|----|--------|-----------|--------|------|--------|
| 1  | ا | جهري ، رخوي ، مستفل ، منفتح ، مصمت | 2 | 3 | ضعيفة |
| 2  | ب | جهري ، شديد ، مستفل ، منفتح ، مذلق ، مقلقل | 3 | 3 | متوسّطة |
| 3  | ت | مهموس ، شديد ، مستفل ، منفتح ، مصمت | 2 | 3 | ضعيفة |
| 4  | ث | مهموس ، رخوي ، مستفل ، منفتح ، مصمت | 1 | 4 | ضعيفة |
| 5  | ج | جهري ، شديد ، مستفل ، منفتح ، مصمت ، مقلقل | 4 | 2 | قويّة |
| 6  | ح | مهموس ، رخوي ، مستفل ، منفتح ، مصمت | 1 | 4 | ضعيفة |
| 7  | خ | مهموس ، رخوي ، مستعل ، منفتح ، مصمت | 2 | 3 | ضعيفة |
| 8  | د | جهري ، شديد ، مستفل ، منفتح ، مصمت ، مقلقل | 4 | 2 | قويّة |
| 9  | ذ | جهري ، رخوي ، مستفل ، منفتح ، مصمت | 2 | 3 | ضعيفة |
| 10 | ر | جهري ، متوسّط ، مستفل ، منفتح ، مذلق ، منحرفة ، مكرر | 3 | 3 | متوسّطة |
| 11 | ز | جهري ، رخوي ، مستفل ، منفتح ، مصمت ، صفيري | 3 | 3 | متوسّطة |
| 12 | س | مهموس ، رخوي ، مستفل ، منفتح ، مصمت ، صفيري | 2 | 4 | ضعيفة |
| 13 | ش | مهموس ، رخوي ، مستفل ، منفتح ، مصمت ، متفشٍّ | 2 | 4 | ضعيفة |

| | | | | | |
|---|---|---|---|---|---|
| 14 | ص | مهموس ، رخوي ، مستعل ، مطبق ، مصمت ، صفيري | 4 | 2 | قويّة |
| 15 | ض | جهري ، رخوي ، مستعل ، مطبق ، مصمت ، مستطيل | 5 | 1 | قويّة |
| 16 | ط | جهري ، شديد ، مستعل ، مطبق ، مصمت ، مقلقل | 6 | 0 | أقوى الحروف |
| 17 | ظ | جهري ، رخوي ، مستعل ، مطبق ، مصمت | 4 | 1 | قويّة |
| 18 | ع | جهري ، متوسّط ، مستفل ، منفتح ، مصمت | 2 | 2 | متوسّطة |
| 19 | غ | جهري ، رخوي ، مستعل ، منفتح ، مصمت | 3 | 2 | قوية |
| 20 | ف | مهموس ، رخوي ، مستفل ، منفتح ، مذلق | 0 | 5 | أضعف الحروف |
| 21 | ق | جهري ، شديد ، مستعل ، منفتح ، مصمت ، مقلقل | 5 | 1 | قويّة |
| 22 | ك | مهموس ، شديد ، مستفل ، منفتح ، مصمت | 2 | 3 | ضعيفة |
| 23 | ل | جهري ، متوسّط ، مستفل ، منفتح ، مذلق ، منحرفة | 2 | 3 | ضعيفة |
| 24 | م | جهري ، متوسّط ، مستفل ، منفتح ، مذلق ، غنّة | 2 | 3 | ضعيفة |
| 25 | ن | جهري ، متوسّط ، مستفل ، منفتح ، مذلق ، غنّة | 2 | 3 | ضعيفة |
| 26 | و | جهري ، رخوي ، مستفل ، منفتح ، مصمت | 2 | 3 | ضعيفة |
| 27 | ه | مهموس ، رخوي ، مستفل ، منفتح ، مصمت | 1 | 4 | ضعيفة |
| 28 | ء | جهري ، شديد ، مستفل ، منفتح ، مصمت | 3 | 2 | قويّة |
| 29 | ي | جهري ، رخوي ، مستفل ، منفتح ، مصمت | 2 | 3 | ضعيفة |

**Notes**:

- The strongest letter is ط (it possesses no weaknesses).
- The weakest letter is ف (it possesses no strengths).

According to the discussion in the chapter of 'qualities' each letter has a certain degree of strength (as indicated in the previous table).

The following table shows the strengths of the different letters, starting with the strongest letter:

|  | Letters | Strength |
|---|---|---|
| 1 | ط | أقوى |
| 2 | ض ، ق | قويّ |
| 3 | ظ | |
| 4 | ج ، د ، ص | |
| 5 | غ ، ء | |
| 6 | ب ، ر ، ز ، ع | متوسّط |
| 7 | ا ، ت ، ذ ، خ ، ك ، ل ، م ، ن ، و ، ي | ضعيف |
| 8 | س ، ش | |
| 9 | ث ، ح ، هـ | |
| 10 | ف ، | أضعف |

# Differences of the letters

According to the مخارج and the صفات learnt, the differences of each letter from another can be learnt. Firstly, most letters are differentiated by their مخارج, however there are some letters which have the same مخرج, hence they are differentiated by their صفات.

The following table mentions the differences between the صفات of the letters with similar مخرج:

| | Letter | Place of Pronunciation | Title | Qualities Same Qualities | Different Qualities |
|---|---|---|---|---|---|
| 1 | الحروف المدّة | الجوف | الحروف الجَوْفِيَّة | جهري ، رخوي ، مستفل ، منفتح ، مصمت | |
| 2 | ء | أقصى الحلق | | مستفل ، منفتح ، مصمت | جهري ، شديد |
| 3 | ه | | | | مهموس ، رخوي |
| 4 | ع | وسط الحلق | الحروف الحَلْقِيَّة | مستفل ، منفتح ، مصمت | جهري ، متوسّط |
| 5 | ح | | | | مهموس ، رخوي |
| 6 | غ | أدنى الحلق | | رخوي ، مستعل ، منفتح ، مصمت | جهري |
| 7 | خ | | | | مهموس |
| 8 | ق | أقصى اللسان وما يحاذيه من الحنك الأعلى | الحروف اللَّهوِيَّة | شديد ، منفتح ، مصمت | جهري ، مستعل ، مقلقل |
| 9 | ك | أقصى اللسان وما يحاذيه من الحنك الأعلى تحت مخرج القاف | | | مهموس ، مستفل |
| 10 | ج | وسط اللسان وما يحاذيه من الحنك الأعلى | الحروف الشَّجَرِيَّة | مستفل ، منفتح ، مصمت | جهري ، شديد ، مقلقل |
| 11 | ش | | | | مهموس ، رخوي ، متفشّي |
| 12 | ض | إحدى حافتي اللسان وما يحاذيه من الأضراس العليا | الحروف الحَافِيَّة | | جهري ، رخوي ، مستعل ، مطبق ، مصمت ، مستطيل |
| 13 | ل | حافة اللسان معا بعد مخرج الضاد وما يحاذيها من اللثة | | | منحرفة |
| 14 | ن | طرف اللسان وما يحاذيه من لثة الأسنان العليا تحت مخرج اللام قليلا | الحروف الذَّلْقِيَّة (الحروف الطرفيّة) | جهري ، متوسّط ، مستفل ، منفتح ، مذلق | غنّة |
| 15 | ر | طرف اللسان مع ظهره مما يلي رأسه وما يحاذيه من لثة الأسنان العليا تحت مخرج النون قليلا | | | منحرفة ، مكرّر |

| | | | | |
|---|---|---|---|---|
| 16 | ت | طرف اللسان مع أصل الثنيتين العليين | الحروف النِطْعِيَّة | شديد ، مصمت | مهموس ، مستفل ، منفتح |
| 17 | د | | | | جهري ، مستفل ، منفتح ، مقلقل |
| 18 | ط | | | | جهري ، مستعل ، مطبق ، مقلقل |
| 19 | ث | طرف اللسان مع طرفي الثنيتين العليين | الحروف اللِثَوِيَّة | رخوي ، مصمت | مهموس ، مستفل ، منفتح |
| 20 | ذ | | | | جهري ، مستفل ، منفتح |
| 21 | ظ | | | | جهري ، مستعل ، مطبق |
| 22 | ز | طرف اللسان مع طرفي الثنيّتين العلييّن و السفلتين معا | الحروف الأَسَلِيَّة | رخوي ، مصمت ، صفيري | جهري ، مستفل ، منفتح |
| 23 | س | | | | مهموس ، مستفل ، منفتح |
| 24 | ص | | | | مهموس ، مستعل ، مطبق |
| 25 | ف | بطن الشفة السفلى مع طرفي الثنيتين العليين | الحروف الشَّفَوِيَّة | مستفل ، منفتح ، مذلق | مهموس ، رخوي |
| 26 | ب | الشفتان معا | | | جهري ، شديد ، مقلقل |
| 27 | م | | | | جهري ، متوسّط ، غنَّة |

**Notes**: The English explanation for the 'place of pronunciation' and 'qualities' have been discussed previously in the relevant chapters.

# Temporary Qualities

The letters in Arabic have certain 'qualities' when pronouncing them. A detailed discussion upon the different 'compulsory qualities' of each letter was mentioned earlier.

Now, the different الصفات العارضة ('temporary qualities') of each letter will be discussed.

'Temporary qualities' are divided into **four** types (causes).

- اللازمة (**compulsory**)
- الاتصال (**joining**)
- الخفاء (**hiding**)
- وضع اللفظ (**formation of the word**)

All four types will be defined when discussing the relevant chapters in detail; however, a brief explanation of each type is given below.

# Brief explanation of the four 'Temporary qualities'

| | Type | Definition |
|---|---|---|
| 1 | لازمة | This is a 'quality' which is **compulsory** in most letters. Therefore, it could be merged into the earlier chapters of 'compulsory qualities'. This chapter discusses two 'opposite qualities'; the 'quality' of تفخيم and ترقيق. Twenty-six letters are fixed in which 'quality' they possess; however, three letters, (ر)(ل)(ا) are **not** fixed with a specific 'quality'. They interchange between the two 'qualities' depending on further rules. These rules will be discussed in the chapters of 'full mouth & empty mouth'. |
| 2 | اتصال | This is a 'quality' which discusses how one letter will be prayed when **joined** with certain other letters; it discusses the 'temporary qualities' that will be formed when joining certain letters together. More detail regarding these chapters will be discussed in the chapters of; *izhaar, idghaam, iqlaab, ikhfaa, madd, noon saakin & tanween, meem saakin & tanween*. |
| 3 | خفاء | This is a 'quality' which discusses **extra softness** that is created whilst reciting certain letters. The dictionary meaning of the word is 'hiding'; this indicates to the **softness** of the voice when reciting these certain letters; almost hiding them. The letters are (ه) and the 'three letters of *madd*'; **remembered with the mnemonic** هاوي. Some scholars have also added the letter (ء) within this 'quality', others have added the letter (ب) within this 'quality'. From amongst the 'letters of *madd*', *alif* is recited the softest, then *yaa* and then *waaw*. The letter (ه) is regarded very weak, yet stronger than the 'three letters of *madd*'. This 'quality' will be discussed randomly throughout the book; mainly in the chapters of the 'pronoun' (ه) and ءِ... |
| 4 | وضع اللفظ | This is a 'quality' which every word possesses; regarding which *harakah* is placed on each letter. All letters originally have a *saakin* upon it, however, the grammarians and linguists of Arabic language formed different words by placing different *harakaat* upon the different letters, also giving some letters a *tashdeed*. This is a 'temporary quality' given to each letter, hence discussed under the chapter of 'temporary qualities'. However, this discussion is not discussed within this book as it is not a subject of 'Qura'nic recitation'; these formations can be searched in grammer books. The discussion of reciting *saakin*, the different *harakaat* and *tashdeed* will be mentioned under the title 'method of reciting the different *harakaat*'. |

# First type of 'temporary qualities – 'لازمة'

There were four types of الصفات العارضة ('temporary qualities') mentioned. The first type was labelled 'اللازمة' ('compulsory quality'). As the name of this 'quality' suggest, this is exactly the same name given to the 'opposite quality' of 'temporary qualities'. The reason this 'temporary quality' is labelled 'compulsory' is because 26 out of the 29 letters possess a **fixed quality** within this type, only 3 letters **do not have a 'fixed quality'** in this chapter, as the following pages outline.

This chapter covers **two** 'qualities':
- التفخيم (full mouth)
- الترقيق (empty mouth)

There were two 'qualities' mentioned before in the section of الصفات المتضادّة (a type of the 'fixed qualities').
The two 'qualities' were:
- الاستعلاء
- الاستفال

The table below recaps their definitions and the letters they represent:

|   | Type | Definition | Letters |   |
|---|------|------------|---------|---|
| 1 | الاستعلاء | **Dictionary**: 'to be raised'<br>**Terminology**: The tongue is 'raised', touching the upper palate of the mouth whilst reciting the letter. | خُصَّ ضَغْطٍ قِظْ | 7 |
| 2 | الاستفال | **Dictionary**: 'to be lowered'<br>**Terminology**: The tongue is 'lowered', not touching the upper palate of the mouth whilst reciting the letter. | ثَبَتَ عِزُّ مَنْ يُجَوِّدُ حَرْفَهُ إِذْ سَلَّ شَكَا | 22 |

## Full mouth & empty mouth

There are two other 'qualities' which are similar to the two mentioned above. They are

- التَّفْخِيْم
- التَّرْقِيْق

The table below defines each type and mentions the letters they represent:

|   | Type | Definition | Letters |   |
|---|------|------------|---------|---|
| 1 | التفخيم | **Dictionary**: 'to magnify' <br> **Terminology**: The letter is magnified to such an extent that whilst reciting the letter, the voice fills the mouth. | خُصَّ ضَغْطٍ قِظْ | 7 |
| 2 | الترقيق | **Dictionary**: 'to make thin' <br> **Terminology**: The letter is made thin to such an extent that whilst reciting the letter, the voice does not fill the mouth. | ثَبَتَ عِزُّ مَنْ يُجَوِّدُ حَفَهُ إِذْ سَ شَكَ | 19 |

In total 7 letters have the 'quality of تفخيم' and 19 letters have the 'quality of ترقيق'.

The letters of تفخيم are **exactly the same** as the letters of استعلاء.

Also, the letters of ترقيق are **exactly the same** as the letters of استفال ; with the **exception of three letters**. The 3 letters are (ا)(ل)(ر). These 3 letters are sometimes prayed with the 'quality of تفخيم' and sometimes with the 'quality of ترقيق'.

They have more detailed rules. It must be understood here that because of these 3 letters and there interchanging between these two 'qualities', the '**qualities**' of تفخيم and ترقيق were **not added** in the category of 'fixed qualities'; instead it was added into the category of 'temporary qualities'.

As 26 out of the 29 letters are in reality fixed, only 3 letters are temporary; the name given to this type of 'temporary qualities' is اللازمة (compulsory qualities). The name given is based upon the majority of the letters, excluding the 3 interchanging letters.

**Note**:

The name الصفات اللازمة is given to the type opposite to الصفات العارضة, it is also the name given to the first type of الصفات العارضة (as discussed above); therefore extra attention should be given to the usage of the two types of الصفات اللازمة.

## Rules of the letter *Alif*

In the discussion of 'full mouth & empty mouth' *alif* was one of the letters that was not mentioned in a category; instead it interchanges between the 'qualities' depending on the following detailed rules in the table below.

| | Type of *Alif* | Rule | Example |
|---|---|---|---|
| 1 | تفخيم (ا) | *Alif* will be read with a **'full mouth'** if the letter before it is from amongst the letters of تفخيم. | قَالَ ، طَالَ |
| 2 | ترقيق (ا) | *Alif* will be read with an **'empty mouth'** if the letter before it is from amongst the letters of ترقيق. | زَالَ ، عَالِيَة |

## Rules of the letter *Laam*

In the discussion of 'full mouth & empty mouth' *laam* was one of the letters that was not mentioned in a category; instead it interchanges between the 'qualities'. **However, this interchanging is only specific with one type of *laam*, the *laam* in the word الله** ; all other types of *laam* possess the 'quality of ترقيق' (empty mouth).

The table below mentions the rules of the *laam* of الله with examples:

| | Type of *Laam* | Rule | Example |
|---|---|---|---|
| 1 | تفخيم (ل) | The *laam* of الله will be read with a **'full mouth'** if the letter before it has a *fathah* or a *dhammah* upon it. | مِنَ اللهِ ، عَلَيْهُ اللهُ |
| 2 | ترقيق (ل) | The *laam* of الله will be read with an **'empty mouth'** if the letter before it has a *kasrah* upon it. | بِسْمِ اللهِ |

## Rules of the letter *Raa*

In the discussion of 'full mouth & empty mouth' *raa* was one of the letters that was not mentioned in a category; instead it interchanges between the 'qualities' depending on the following detailed rules.

Firstly, there are two situations for all letters; the state of **continuing** (وصل) recitation upon a letter and the state of **stopping** (وقف) upon a letter.

Similarly, in the letter *raa* these two possibilities are present, depending on whether the reader continues recitation beyond the letter *raa* or the reader stops/pauses on the letter *raa*, there will be different rules.

### The rules for the letter *Raa* when continuing the recitation

The 'letter *raa* when continuing the recitation' will be read with a '**full mouth**' except in three situations; it will be read with an '**empty mouth**'.

The table below mentions with an example the situations when the '*raa* in continued recitation' will be read with an '**empty mouth**':

| | Rules | Example |
|---|---|---|
| 1 | When the *raa* itself has a *kasrah* upon it (This can be any type of *kasrah*; original or temporary)*. | رِجَال ، غَارِمِيْنَ ، أَنْذِرِ النَّاسَ |
| 2 | When the *raa* itself has a *saakin* & the letter **directly prior** to it has an **original** *kasrah* and no 'full mouth letters with a *fathah* or *dhammah*' occur **directly after** it. | فِرْعَوْنُ ، شِرْعَة |
| 3 | When the *raa* is prayed with إِمَالَة**. | مَجْرِبهَا |

* An original *kasrah* is when the letter originally (before any grammatical changes) possesses the *kasrah*, for example the word رِجال , the *kasrah* on the *raa* is original. However, if the *raa* does not have a *kasrah* originally, it gets a *kasrah* later due to grammatical rules; this is called a 'temporary *kasrah*'. The *raa* in the phrase أنذِرِ الناس has a 'temporary *kasrah*'; it was originally a *saakin*.

** إِمَالَة is when a letter has a *fathah*, but it is prayed with a *fathah-kasrah* mixture; or when the letter is an *alif*, but it is prayed with an *alif-yaa* mixture.

The table below mentions with an example the situations when the *'raa* in continued recitation' will be read with a '**full mouth**', as it does not agree with the three conditions for '**empty mouth** *raa*' mentioned above:

|  | Situation | Example |
|---|---|---|
| 1 | When the *raa* has a *fathah* upon it. | رَبَّنَا |
| 2 | When the *raa* has a *dhammah* upon it. | رُسُل |
| 3 | When the *raa* has a *saakin* which has a *fathah* prior to it. | بَرْق |
| 4 | When the *raa* has a *saakin* which has a *dhammah* prior to it. | الْقُرْآن |
| 5 | When the *raa* has a *saakin* which has a **temporary** *kasrah* prior to it. | ارْجِعِي |
| 6 | When the *raa* has a *saakin* which has a **detached** *kasrah* prior to it (detached is indicating to when the *kasrah* is not directly before the *raa*). | الَّذِيْ ارْتَضَى |
| 7 | When the *raa* has a *saakin* which has one of the 'full mouth letters' occurring **directly** after it and the 'full mouth letter' **does not** have a *kasrah* upon it. | قِرْطَاس |

**Notes**:

(1) The situation where there is a 'full mouth letter' after *raa saakin* and the 'full mouth letter' is **not** *kasrah* is limited to five words in the Qur'an. They are:

( قِرْطَاس )[الأنعام:7]( إِرْصَاد )[التوبة:107]( فِرْقَة )[التوبة:122]( مِرْصَاد )[النبأ:21]( لَبِالْمِرْصَاد )[الفجر:14]

(2) If the *raa saakin* has a 'full mouth letter' after it, which is in the next word, the *raa* will be read with an **empty mouth** if all the conditions of 'empty mouth *raa*' are met.

Example: (فَاصْبِرْ صَبْرًا) [المعارج:5] and (لَا تُصَعِّرْ خَدَّك) [لقمان:18], in these two examples even though the *raa* has a *saakin* with a 'full mouth letter' occurring after it; it will still be read with an '**empty mouth**' as the 'full mouth letter' is detached, in the next word.

(3) If the *raa saakin* has a 'full mouth letter' **directly** after it, however it has a *kasrah* upon it, then it is permissible to pray such a *raa saakin* with an 'empty mouth' or 'full mouth'. However, scholars mention that it is better to pray it with an '**empty mouth**'.

Example: (فِرْقٍ) [الشعراء:63], in this word as there is a *raa saakin* with one of the 'full mouth letters' occurring directly after it, it is permissible to pray 'full mouth'. However, as the 'full mouth letter' itself has a *kasrah* upon it, it is also permissible to pray the letter (ر) with an 'empty mouth'. **However, praying it with an 'empty mouth' will be better.**

The rules for *Raa* when stopping/pausing (وَقْف)

The 'letter *raa* when stopping/pausing upon it' will be read with a **'full mouth'** except in three situations; it will be read with an **'empty mouth'**.

The table below mentions with an example the situations when the 'letter *raa* when stopping/pausing upon it' will be read with an **'empty mouth'**:

|   | Situation | Example |
|---|---|---|
| 1 | If **directly before** the *raa* there is a *kasrah*. | بَصَائِرْ |
| 2 | If before the *raa* there is a *saakin* letter from amongst the 'empty mouth letters' and has a *kasrah* preceding it. | سِحْرْ ، الذِّكْرْ |
| 3 | If **directly** before the *raa* there is a *yaa saakin*. | قَدِيرْ ، الْخَيْرْ |

The table below mentions with an example the situations when the 'letter *raa* when stopping/pausing upon it' will be read with a **'full mouth'**, as it does not agree with the three conditions for **'empty mouth *raa*'** mentioned above:

|   | Situation | Example |
|---|---|---|
| 1 | If the letter prior to the *raa* has a *fathah*. | الْقَمَرْ |
| 2 | If the letter prior to the *raa* has a *dhammah*. | النُّذُرْ |
| 3 | If the letter prior to the *raa* is a *saakin* letter from the 'empty mouth letters' and the letter before this has a *fathah*. | الْفَجْرْ |

**Notes**:

(1) The rulings regarding the 'letter *raa* when stopping/pausing upon it' is specific with certain types of *waqf* ; the rules will apply in the state of الوقف بالإسكان and الوقف بالإشمام , not in the state of الوقف بالروم. The detailed discussion on *waqf* will be discussed later in the book.

(2) If the 'letter *raa* when stopping/pausing upon it' has a *'saakin* full mouth letter' directly prior to it, preceded by a *kasrah*, then it is permissible to pray the *raa* with a 'full mouth' or an 'empty mouth'.

However, scholars mention that if the *raa* originally had a *fathah* or *dhammah* upon it, then it is better to pray it with a 'full mouth'. If the *raa* originally had a *kasrah* upon it, then it is better to pray it with an 'empty mouth'.

Examples:

1. The word (مِصْرَ) [يونس:87] , as the *raa* has a *saakin* when you stop upon it and the letter prior to it also has a *saakin*, and this letter is from amongst the 'full mouth letters'; it is permissible to pray the *raa* with a 'full mouth' or an 'empty mouth', however it is **better** to pray the *raa* with a 'full mouth' because the *raa* originally had a *fathah* upon it.

2. The word (الْقِطْرِ) [السبا:12] , as the *raa* has a *saakin* when you stop upon it and the letter prior to it also has a *saakin*, and this letter is from amongst the 'full mouth letters'; it is permissible to pray the *raa* with a 'full mouth' or an 'empty mouth', however it is **better** to pray the *raa* with an 'empty mouth' because the *raa* originally had a *kasrah* upon it.

(3) There are three words within the Qur'an which end with the letter *raa* which, according to the above rules, when stopping/pausing should be read with a 'full mouth'; however scholars have mentioned that these three words alone can be read with a full mouth or an 'empty mouth'; it is **better** to pray it with an 'empty mouth', indicating upon a **hidden *yaa*** after the letter *raa* in these words. The three words are:

( يَسْرِ )[الفجر:4]( أَسْرِ )[طه:77]( نُذُرِ )[القمر:16 ، 18 ، 21 ، 30 ، 37 ، 39]

In these words, according to the rules the letter *raa* should be read with a 'full mouth' when stopping/pausing.

(4) If the *raa* has a *tashdeed* upon it, the rules applied will be exactly the same as the *non-tashdeed raa* ; the rules mentioned above will be applied in both situations.

# Levels of 'full mouth' recitation

There were seven letters mentioned in the 'full mouth' recitation 'quality'. However, each letter has a different level of 'full mouth' recitation depending on what situation it occurs in, these levels determine the strength and weakness of the 'quality' of 'full mouth' within the letter at that given time.

The table below indicates to the strength of the 'full mouth' letters with an example:

| | | Type | Example |
|---|---|---|---|
| 1 | Strongest | When the letter has a *fathah* upon it and after it there is an *alif*. | طَائِعُوْنَ |
| 2 | | When the letter has a *fathah* upon it and after it there is no *alif*. | طَلَبًا |
| 3 | | When the letter has a *dhammah*. | يَسْطُرُوْن |
| 4 | | When the letter has a *saakin*. | أَطْعَمَهُمْ |
| 5 | Weakest | When the letter has a *kasrah*. | طِبْتُمْ |

**Notes**:

(1) Certain scholars have mentioned that the *saakin* type is not individually regarded within the 'full mouth' strength list; instead its strength follows the *harakah* of the letter before.
Example: The word [4:قريش] (أَطْعَمَهُمْ) will have the same strength as the second type; when the letter has a *fathah* upon it and after it there is no *alif*.

(2) It is important to make sure the 'full mouth' strengths are considered when praying the letters, it is **disliked** to pray a weaker letter strongly, and vice versa.
If the words are prayed with different strengths then the *harakaat*, etc could change.

(3) It is **not permissible** to pray an 'empty mouth' *raa* with such strength that it becomes إِمَالَة .

# Second type of 'temporary qualities – اتّصال'

There were four types of الصفات العارضة ('temporary qualities') mentioned. The second type was labelled 'الاتّصال' (joint). This 'quality' is regarding whether the reciter would join two letters together or not whilst reciting them, also it discusses how the letters of *madd* are pronounced and joint.

However, the chapter on *madd* will not be discussed here, instead it will be discussed in a later, separate chapter. The 'quality' of joining (or not joining) two letters will be discussed in this chapter.

The overall chapter will discuss three main situations of joining (or not joining) two letters together. The three situations are:

1. الإظهار – separating the two letters in pronunciation.
2. الإدغام – joining the two letters in pronunciation.
3. الإخفاء – partially joining the two letters in pronunciation,
   (only joining them in 'qualities', not 'place of pronunciation').

This chapter will outline these three 'qualities', however as the rules of *noon saakin* & *tanween* are also dominant in this discussion, it will be discussed separately.

## Noon Saakin and Tanween

The following table defines *'noon saakin & tanween'*:

| | Type | Definition | Example |
|---|---|---|---|
| 1 | **Noon Saakin** | It is such a *noon* which **does not have** any *harakah* upon it. | مِنْ ، عَنْ |
| 2 | **Tanween** | It is an **extra *noon saakin*** at the end of a word, which is **present** in **reciting** but **not present** in **writing** or when pausing upon the *noon*. | فَلَقٍ |

**Notes**:

(1) A *noon saakin* can appear in a **noun** or a **verb**, it can also occur **inbetween** a word or at the **end** of a word.

(2) *Tanween* is discussed together with *noon saakin* because *tanween* is a type of *noon saakin* despite a *noon* not being present in **writing**.

(3) More rules regarding *tanween* will be discussed later.

## Rules of 'Noon Saakin and Tanween':

In terms of the different letters occurring after 'noon saakin and tanween', there are **four** different rules:

- الإظْهَار
- الإدْغَام
- الإخْفَاء
- الإقْلَاب

<u>Note</u>: The extra quality of إقلاب has been added in this discussion, the table below will define this type.

The table below defines the four types:

|   | Term | Definition |
|---|---|---|
| 1 | الإظْهَار | **Dictionary**: 'to express' <br> **Terminology**: A 'quality' in which each letter is 'expressed' from its own 'place of pronunciation' **without *ghunnah***. |
| 2 | الإدْغَام | **Dictionary**: 'to make enter' <br> **Terminology**: A 'quality' in which one *saakin* letter is made to 'enter' into the following *mutaharrik* letter; making them into one *mushaddad* letter. |
| 3 | الإخْفَاء | **Dictionary**: 'to hide' <br> **Terminology**: A 'quality' in which the letter is prayed between *izhaar* and *idghaam*; it will **not** change into a *mushaddad* letter but there **will be *ghunnah***. |
| 4 | الإقْلَاب | **Dictionary**: 'to change' <br> **Terminology**: A 'quality' in which one *saakin* letter is 'changed' into another letter; the *noon saakin* or *tanween* will be changed into the letter *baa*. |

The rule of *Izhaar* for '*Noon Saakin* and *Tanween*':

If one of the letters from amongst الْحُرُوْف الْحَلْقِيَّة occur after a *noon saakin* or *tanween*, *izhaar* will occur. Therefore, the *noon saakin* or *tanween* will be pronounced **clearly, without ghunnah;** the following letter which is from amongst الحروف الحلقيّة will also be pronounced **clearly, without ghunnah**.

This *izhaar* is called الإظْهَار الْحَلْقِيّ (*Izhaar-ul Halqi*) because the letters are from الْحُرُوْف الْحَلْقِيَّة.

The **reason** for *izhaar* in these words is the far distance between the 'places of pronunciation' for the letter *noon* and الحروف الحلقيّة. The *noon* is pronounced when the edge of the tongue joins the gums (near the front of the mouth); and الحروف الحلقيّة are pronounced from the throat.

The following table gives examples of '*noon saakin* and *tanween*' occurring before the six different الحروف الحلقيّة:

|   | الحروف الحلقيّة | Example with *Noon Saakin* in the same word | Example with *Noon Saakin* in a different word | Example with *Tanween* |
|---|---|---|---|---|
| 1 | ا | يَنْأَوْنَ | مِنْ أَجْرٍ | كُلٌّ آمَنَ |
| 2 | هـ | مُنْهَمِر | مِنْ هَادٍ | فَرِيْقًا هَدَى |
| 3 | ع | أَنْعَمْتَ | مِنْ عِلْمٍ | حَكِيْمٌ عَلِيْمٌ |
| 4 | ح | يَنْحِتُوْنَ | مِنْ حَكِيْمٍ | حَكِيْمٌ حَمِيْدٌ |
| 5 | غ | فَسَيُنْغِضُوْنَ | مِنْ غِلٍّ | قَوْلًا غَيْرَ |
| 6 | خ | الْمُنْخَنِقَة | مِنْ خَيْرٍ | يَوْمَئِذٍ خَاشِعَةٌ |

**Note**: Tanween will **never** occur inbetween a word.

50

The rule of *Idghaam* for *'Noon Saakin* and *Tanween'*:

If one of the letters of (ي)(ر)(م)(ل)(و)(ن) occur after a *noon saakin* or *tanween* then *idghaam* will occur. However, with some letters when *idghaam* occurs *ghunnah* will also occur; and with some letters of *idghaam*, *ghunnah* **will not** occur.

The following table mentions the two types of *idghaam* and mentions the letters for each type:

|   | Type | Explanation | Letters |
|---|------|-------------|---------|
| 1 | الإدْغَام بِالْغُنَّة<br>*Idghaam* with *ghunnah* | *Ghunnah* **will** occur whilst doing *idghaam*. | يَنْمُوْ (ي)(ن)(م)(و) |
| 2 | الإدْغَام بِغَيْرِ الْغُنَّة<br>*Idghaam* without *ghunnah* | *Ghunnah* **will not** occur whilst doing *idghaam*. | (ل)(ر) |

**Note**: The letters (ي)(ر)(م)(ل)(و)(ن) can be remembered with the mnemonic يَرْمَلُوْنَ.

## The rule of 'Idghaam with Ghunnah' for 'Noon Saakin and Tanween':

If one of the **four letters** from (ي)(ن)(م)(و) occur after a *noon Saakin* or *tanween* there will be '*idghaam* with *ghunnah*'. However, this '*idghaam* with *ghunnah*' **only occurs if the noon saakin or tanween occurs at the end of the word** with one of the four letters from (ي)(ن)(م)(و) at the beginning of the next word.

The following table mentions examples of '*idghaam* with *ghunnah*' for the four letters:

| | Letter | Example with *Noon Saakin* | Example with *Tanween* |
|---|---|---|---|
| 1 | ي | مَنْ يَقُوْلُ | وُجُوْهٌ يَوْمَئِذٍ |
| 2 | ن | مِنْ نِّعْمَةٍ | يَوْمَئِذٍ نَّاعِمَةٌ |
| 3 | م | مِنْ مَّاءٍ | سُرُرٌ مَّرْفُوْعَةٌ |
| 4 | و | مِنْ وَّلِيٍّ | نَعِيْمًا وَّمُلْكًا |

**Notes**:

(1) If one of the letters from (ي)(ن)(م)(و) occur after a *noon saakin* in the **same word** then *idghaam* will **not** occur, instead *izhaar* will occur. This occurs in **four words** within the Qur'an:

| | Word |
|---|---|
| 1 | الدُّنْيَا [البقرة:85] |
| 2 | بُنْيَان [التوبة:109] |
| 3 | قِنْوَان [الأنعام:99] |
| 4 | صِنْوَان [الرعد:4] |

This *izhaar* is called الْإِظْهَار الْمُطْلَق (unrestricted *izhaar*) because the letters are **not** restricted to the throat or lips.

The reason for *izhaar* in these words is that if *idghaam* occurred, the reader or listener could get **confused**; was the original a *noon saakin* or was it originally a double letter.

Example: In the word بُنْيّ if *idghaam* is done then it will become بُيّ, this could cause confusion whether it is a double *yaa* or it was originally a *noon saakin*.

(2) If a reciter joins the verses of [ وَالْقُرْآنِ ۝1 يٰسٓ ] or [ وَالْقَلَمِ ۝1 نٓ ] together, then according to the rules mentioned above there should be '*idghaam* with *ghunnah*' occurring; as the *noon saakin* is occurring at the end of the first word and the letter *waaw* is occurring at the beginning of the second word. However, the famous view is to do *izhaar* in this situation, **not** '*idghaam* with *ghunnah*'; some scholars mention '*idghaam* with *ghunnah*' will occur.

(3) The letters (ي)(ن)(م)(و) can be remembered with the mnemonic يَنْمُوْ.

## The rule of '*Idghaam* without *Ghunnah*' for '*Noon Saakin* and *Tanween*'

If one of the letters ر or ل occur after a *noon saakin* or *tanween* there will be '*idghaam* without *ghunnah*'.

The following table mentions examples of '*idghaam* without *ghunnah*' for the two letters:

|   | Letter | Example with *Noon Saakin* | Example with *Tanween* |
|---|---|---|---|
| 1 | ر | مِنْ رَّبِّهِمْ | غَفُوْرًا رَّحِيْمًا |
| 2 | ل | مِنْ لَّدُنْهُ | رَحْمَةً لِّلْعَالَمِيْنَ |

**Notes**:

(1) There is no example within the Qur'an when there is *noon saakin* and the next letter is the letter ل or the letter ر within the same word.

(2) There is a difference of opinion amongst scholars regarding doing *ghunnah* when one of the letters ر or ل occur after a *noon saakin*; the **famous view** is to do '*idghaam* without *ghunnah*' (as mentioned above), however some scholars have mentioned that in this case '*idghaam* with *ghunnah*' will occur when the *noon saakin* is present in writing; if the *noon saakin* is not present in writing then similar to the famous view they also do '*idghaam* without *ghunnah*'.

Example: In the chapter of *Hud* verse 26 (أَنْ لَّا تَعْبُدُوْا إِلَّا اللّٰهَ) as the *noon saakin* is written '*idghaam* with *ghunnah*' is done; however, in the chapter of *Hud* verse 2 (أَلَّا تَعْبُدُوْا إِلَّا اللّٰهَ) '*idghaam* without *ghunnah*' is done as the *noon saakin* is **not written**.

## Complete or incomplete *Idghaam*

There are two types of *idghaam* in terms of 'quality':

(1) Complete *idghaam* – this is called الْإِدْغَامُ الْكَامِلُ.

(2) Incomplete *idghaam* – this is called الْإِدْغَامُ النَّاقِصُ.

The following table defines each type of *idghaam*:

|   | Type | Definition |
|---|------|------------|
| 1 | Complete *Idghaam* | This is when the first letter has **completely** merged into the second letter; the letter & its 'qualities' have merged. Now, the second letter will be pronounced as a double letter. |
| 2 | Incomplete *Idghaam* | This is when the first letter has **incompletely** merged into the second letter; the letter has merged but not its 'qualities'. Now, the second letter will be pronounced as a double letter, however the 'quality of *ghunnah*' for the *noon saakin* will remain. |

From the **six letters** mentioned above, (ي)(و)(م)(ل)(و)(ن), the scholars have agreed that with *noon saakin*:

- **Two letters** (و)(ي) **will have incomplete *idghaam*** because the 'quality of *ghunnah*' which is from the *noon saakin* will remain.

  Example: When pronouncing [البقرة:8] مَنْ يَقُوْلُ , the 'quality of *ghunnah*' within the *noon saakin* will remain despite the letter *noon* merging into the letter *yaa*.

- **Two letters** (ر)(ل) **will have complete *idghaam*** because the 'quality of *ghunnah*' which is from the *noon saakin* does not remain.

  Example: When pronouncing [البقرة:5] مِنْ رَّبِّهِمْ , the 'quality of *ghunnah*' within the *noon saakin* will not remain despite the letter *noon* merging into the letter *raa*.

However, the scholars have different views regarding the other **two letters**, (م) and (ن);

- Some say the 'quality of *ghunnah*' from the *noon saakin* is still left when merging it into the second letter, the *meem* or *noon*; **hence** الإدغام الناقص.

- Most scholars' say the 'quality of *ghunnah*' present is from the second letter, meaning the *noon* or the *meem*; the 'quality of *ghunnah*' is **not** from the *noon saakin*. The *noon saakin* along with **all** its 'qualities' have been removed and merged **completely** into the second letter; **hence** الإدغام الكامل.

Note: There are different types of *idghaam* depending on how close the 'place of pronunciation' and the 'qualities' of the letters are. These types will be discussed later in detail.

## The rule of *Iqlaab* for *'Noon Saakin* and *Tanween'*

If the letter *baa*, occurs after a *noon saakin* or *tanween*, *iqlaab* will occur. The *noon saakin* or *tanween* will change into the letter *meem*. In this case *ikhfaa* and *ghunnah* will occur.

The following table gives examples of *'noon saakin* and *tanween'* occurring before the letter *baa*:

|   | Letter | Example with *Noon Saakin* in the same word | Example with *Noon Saakin* in a different word | Example with *Tanween* |
|---|---|---|---|---|
| 1 | ب | أَنْبِئْهُمْ | أَنْ بُورِكَ | سَمِيعٌ بَصِيرٌ |

**Note**: The reason for changing the *'noon saakin* and *tanween'* specifically to the letter *meem* is because the letter *meem* is similar to the letter *baa* in terms of 'place of pronunciation' and similar to the letter *noon* in terms of 'qualities of a letter'.

## The rule of *Ikhfaa* for *'Noon Saakin* and *Tanween'*

From amongst the 29 letters of the Arabic alphabet, 13 letters have already been discussed in the other 'qualities'; further, excluding *alif* (as *alif* will **never** occur after *noon saakin* or *tanween*) there will be a total of 15 letters remaining. The 15 letters are:

(ت)(ث)(ج)(د)(ذ)(ز)(س)(ش)(ص)(ض)(ط)(ظ)(ف)(ق)(ك)

When a *noon saakin* or *tanween* occurs before any of these letters, *ikhfaa* will occur.

The following table gives examples of *'noon saakin* and *tanween'* occurring before the letters of *ikhfaa*:

|   | Letter | Example with *Noon Saakin* in the same word | Example with *Noon Saakin* in a different word | Example with *Tanween* |
|---|---|---|---|---|
| 1 | ت | مُنْتَهُوْنَ | مِنْ تَحْتِهَا | جَنَّاتٍ تَجْرِيْ |
| 2 | ث | مَنْثُوْرًا | مِنْ ثَمَرَةٍ | قَلِيْلًا ثُمَّ |
| 3 | ج | أَنْجَيْنَاكُمْ | إِنْ جَاءَكُمْ | صَبْرًا جَمِيْلًا |
| 4 | د | أَنْدَادًا | مِنْ دَابَّةٍ | عَمَلًا دُوْنَ |
| 5 | ذ | مُنْذِرٌ | مِنْ ذِكْرٍ | سِرَاعًا ذَلِكَ |
| 6 | ز | أَنْزَلْنَاهُ | فَإِنْ زَلَلْتُمْ | نَفْسًا زَكِيَّةً |
| 7 | س | مِنْسَأَتَهُ | مِنْ سُلَالَةٍ | سَلَامًا سَلَامًا |
| 8 | ش | الْمُنْشِئُوْنَ | لِمَنْ شَاءَ | غَفُوْرٌ شَكُوْرٌ |
| 9 | ص | مَنْصُوْرًا | أَنْ صَدُّوْكُمْ | عَمَلًا صَالِحًا |
| 10 | ض | مَنْضُوْدٌ | إِنْ ضَلَلْتُ | مُسْفِرَةٌ ضَاحِكَةٌ |
| 11 | ط | يَنْطِقُوْنَ | مِنْ طَيِّبَاتِ | صَعِيْدًا طَيِّبًا |
| 12 | ظ | انْظُرُوْا | مِنْ ظَهِيْرٍ | ظِلًّا ظَلِيْلًا |
| 13 | ف | انْفِرُوْا | مِنْ فَضْلِهِ | سُبُلًا فِجَاجًا |
| 14 | ق | يَنْقَلِبُ | إِنْ قِيْلَ | عَلِيْمًا قَدِيْرًا |
| 15 | ك | مِنْكُمْ | مَنْ كَانَ | نَاصِيَةٍ كَاذِبَةٍ |

**Notes**:

(1) The reason for *ikhfaa* with these letters is that the *noon saakin* (or *tanween*) is **not as close** to these 15 letters as it is close to the 6 letters of *idghaam*, however it is **not as far** from these 15 letters as from the 6 letters of *izhaar*; it is inbetween, hence *ikhfaa*.

(2) There are **three levels** of *ikhfaa* according to how strong or weak the *ikhfaa* is:

| Strongest with the letters | Inbetween with the letters | Weakest with the letters |
|---|---|---|
| (ط)(د)(ت) | (ث)(ج)(ذ)(ز)(س)(ش)(ص)(ض)(ظ)(ف) | (ق)(ك) |

(3) Some scholars have gathered the letters of *ikhfaa* with the following phrase:

$$\text{سَتُجْزَ صَدَّكَ فَثِقْ ضَطَظَ شَذٌّ}$$

57

## Meem Saakin

'Meem saakin' is such a *meem* which does not have any *harakah* upon the *meem*; instead it has a *saakin*. This type of 'meem saakin' can appear in a noun or a verb; similarly, it can occur at the end or inbetween a word.

### Rules of 'Meem Saakin':

In terms of the different letters occurring after 'meem saakin', there are three different rules:
- الإظْهَار
- الإدْغَام
- الإخْفَاء

**Notes:**
(1) The definitions of these types were mentioned at the beginning of the 'noon saakin and tanween' chapter.
(2) There is no *iqlaab* present in the discussion of 'meem saakin'.

The rule of *Idghaam* for *'Meem Saakin'*:

After *'meem saakin'*, if another *meem* appears, *idghaam* will occur. The first letter, the *'meem saakin'* will be completely merged into the following *meem*.

This (*meem*) is the only letter with which *idghaam* occurs with a *'meem saakin'*.

This type of *idghaam* is called الإدْغَام الصَّغِيْر (small *idghaam*) as the changes occurred to the two letters during *idghaam* are **small**, (in this case not present).

This type of *idghaam* is also called الإدغام الشَّفَوِيّ (*idghaam shafawee*) because both the letters are pronounced from the **lips** – in Arabic this is called شَفَة.

The following table gives an example of *'meem saakin'* with a *meem* as the following letter:

|   | Letter | Example with *'Meem Saakin'* in a noun |
|---|--------|----------------------------------------|
| 1 | م      | خَلَقَ لَكُمْ مَا فِيْ الأرض            |

### The rule of *Ikhfaa* for *'Meem Saakin'*:

After *'meem saakin'*, if the letter *baa* appears then *ikhfaa* will occur. The first letter, the *'meem saakin'* will not be merged into the letter *baa*, however *ghunnah* will occur.

This is the only letter with which *ikhfaa* occurs with a *'meem saakin'*.

This type of *ikhfaa* is also called الإخفاء الشَّفَوِيّ because both the letters are pronounced from the **lips**.

The reason for *ikhfaa* in these words is because the 'place of pronunciation' for both letters are the same, however the 'qualities of the letters' are slightly different; hence *ikhfaa* (the inbetween option) occurs.

The following table gives examples of *'meem saakin'* with a *baa* as the following letter:

|   | Letter | Example with *'Meem Saakin'* in a noun | Example with *'Meem Saakin'* in a verb |
|---|--------|----------------------------------------|----------------------------------------|
| 1 | ب | يَوْمَ هُمْ بَارِزُونَ | يَعْتَصِمْ بِاللهِ |

**Notes**:

(1) There is no example in the Qur'an for when the *'meem saakin'* is **inbetween** a word and the following letter is the letter *baa*.

(2) Scholars have differed in opinion whether *ikhfaa* or *izhaar* will occur when the letter *baa* occurs after *'meem saakin'*. Some scholars say 'complete *izhaar*' will occur, therefore, no *ghunnah* will occur. However, most scholars mention that *ikhfaa* will occur, therefore, *ghunnah* will also occur. The scholars who give the opinion of *ikhfaa* give an analogy with the *iqlaab* situation where the *noon saakin* or *tanween* was changed to a *'meem saakin'* before the letter *baa*.

The rule of *Izhaar* for *'Meem Saakin'*:
___

After *'meem saakin'*, if the letters other than *baa* & *meem* occur, there will be *izhaar*. However, the letter *alif* will never occur after *'meem saakin'*. Therefore, in total there are 26 letters that can occur after *'meem saakin'* in which *izhaar* will occur. The 26 letters are:

(ت)(ث)(ج)(ح)(خ)(د)(ذ)(ر)(ز)(س)(ش)(ص)(ض)(ط)(ظ)(ع)(غ)(ف)(ق)(ك)(ل)(ن)(و)(ه)(ء)(ي)

This *izhaar* is called الإظْهار الشَّفَوِيّ because *meem is* pronounced from the **lips**.

The following table gives examples of *'meem saakin'* with a *taa* as the following letter:

|   | Letter | Example with *'Meem Saakin'* in the same word | Example with *'Meem Saakin'* in a different word |
|---|---|---|---|
| 1 | ت | أَنْعَمْتَ | لَعَلَّكُمْ تَتَّقُونَ |

**Notes**:
(1) All the other letters mentioned above will follow the same pronunciation method.
(2) Some reciters prefer to do *ikhfaa* when the letters *waaw* or *faa* occur after *'meem saakin'*. They compare the *waaw* and *faa* to the letter *baa* with which *ikhfaa* is done. The letters *waaw* and *faa* have the same or close 'place of pronunciation' to the letter *baa*; hence, their ruling should also be the same, meaning *ikhfaa* should be done. However, *ikhfaa* of *'meem saakin'* with *waaw* **will not** occur as it could confuse the reader/listener whether the original first letter was a *'meem saakin'* or *'noon saakin'*. Further, *ikhfaa* of *'meem saakin'* into *faa* will not occur because *meem* is a stronger letter than *faa*, (*faa* is the weakest letter); **a stronger letter can never be hidden (do ikhfaa) in a weaker letter;** hence complete & clear *izhaar* will be done.

# Rules of *Ghunnah*

*Ghunnah* is a '**permanent** quality' in which the noise along with the mouth is also produced in the nose. It occurs in two letters; *meem* & *noon*.

There are different levels to the nature of *ghunnah* in the letters *meem* & *noon*. The different levels can be divided into five categories as indicated in the table below:

|   |   | Type | Example with the letter *meem* | Example with the letter *noon* |
|---|---|---|---|---|
| 1 | Strongest | When the letter *meem* or *noon* is *mushaddad*. | لَمَّا جَآءَهُمْ | لَوْ أَنَّهُمْ |
| 2 |   | When *idghaam* has occurred in the letter *meem* or *noon*. | خَلَقَ لَكُمْ مَا | مَنْ يَقُوْلُ |
| 3 |   | When *ikhfaa* has occurred in the letter *meem* or *noon*. | يَعْتَصِمْ بِاللهِ | مِنْ تَحْتِهَا |
| 4 |   | When the letter *meem* or *noon* is *saakin*. |   |   |
| 5 | Weakest | When the letter *meem* or *noon* is *mutaharrik*. |   |   |

**Notes**:

(1) The length of the *ghunnah* in the **first, second & third situation** will be the length of '*two harakaat*' which is equivalent to **two seconds**.

(2) The *ghunnah* will be so weak in the last two situations that the 'quality' of *ghunnah* will not be noticed; instead only the letters *meem* & *noon* will be noticed.

(3) If the *meem* is *mushaddad* or has the letter *baa* after it then *ghunnah* will occur; otherwise it will not occur with the letter *meem*.

(4) If the *noon* is *mushaddad* or has any letter **except** (ل)(ر)(خ)(غ)(ح)(ع)(هـ)(ء) then *ghunnah* will occur; otherwise it will not occur with the letter *noon*.

# Situations of two letters occurring next to each other

## Letters occurring next to each other in terms of pronunciation & qualities

There are four different situations and names given to two letters occurring next to each other in terms of the 'place of pronunciation' and 'qualities' of the letters:

- الْمُتَمَاثِلَانِ
- الْمُتَقَارِبَانِ
- الْمُتَجَانِسَانِ
- الْمُتَبَاعِدَانِ

The table below defines and gives examples of each type:

| | Situation | Definition | Example |
|---|---|---|---|
| 1 | الْمُتَمَاثِلَانِ | **Dictionary**: 'to be identical to the other' <br> **Terminology**: These are two letters occurring next to each other which are **exactly the same letters**, the 'place of pronunciation' and **all** the 'qualities' are the same; this can only occur if the two letters are the same letters. | اذْهَبْ بِكِتَابِي |
| 2 | الْمُتَقَارِبَانِ | **Dictionary**: 'to be close to each other' <br> **Terminology**: These are two letters occurring next to each other which are **close in both**; 'place of pronunciation' and 'qualities'; or close only in the 'place of pronunciation' or close only in the 'qualities' of the letters. | قُلْ رَبِّ |
| 3 | الْمُتَجَانِسَانِ | **Dictionary**: 'to be similar to the other' <br> **Terminology**: These are two letters occurring next to each other which are the **same** in either the 'place of pronunciation' or the 'qualities' of the letters; **they are not the same in both**. | قَدْ تَبَيَّنَ |
| 4 | الْمُتَبَاعِدَانِ | **Dictionary**: 'to be separate from the other' <br> **Terminology**: These are two letters occurring next to each other which are **different to each other in both**; the 'place of pronunciation' and the 'qualities' of the letters. | أَنْعَمْتَ عَلَيْهِمْ |

**Note**: The terms mentioned above for 'two letters occurring next to each other' only considers the **writing of the text**, it does not take into consideration the pronunciation.

The following examples will clarify this point further.

In the phrase [30:الذاريات] إِنَّهُ هُوَ , in writing two *haa*'s are occurring next to each other; however, in pronunciation the letter *waaw* occurs inbetween. Despite the letter *waaw* occurring inbetween the two *haa*'s in pronunciation; this type will be called الْمُتَمَاثِلَانِ **as the writing is considered**, **not the pronunciation**.

On the other hand, in the phrase [50:العنكبوت] أَنَا نَذِيرٌ , in writing there is an *alif* between the two *noon*'s; however, in pronunciation this *alif* is not pronounced, the two *noons* are pronounced next to each other. Despite the two *noons* occurring next to each other in pronunciation; this type will be called الْمُتَبَاعِدَانِ **as the writing will be considered**, **not the pronunciation**.

In the table above a total of **seven** situations are indicated. They are:

- الْمُتَمَاثِلَانِ
- الْمُتَقَارِبَانِ فِي الْمَخْرَجِ والصِّفَةِ مَعًا
- الْمُتَقَارِبَانِ فِي الْمَخْرَجِ فَقَطْ
- الْمُتَقَارِبَانِ فِي الصِّفَةِ فَقَطْ
- الْمُتَجَانِسَانِ فِي الْمَخْرَجِ فَقَطْ
- الْمُتَجَانِسَانِ فِي الصِّفَةِ فَقَطْ
- الْمُتَبَاعِدَانِ

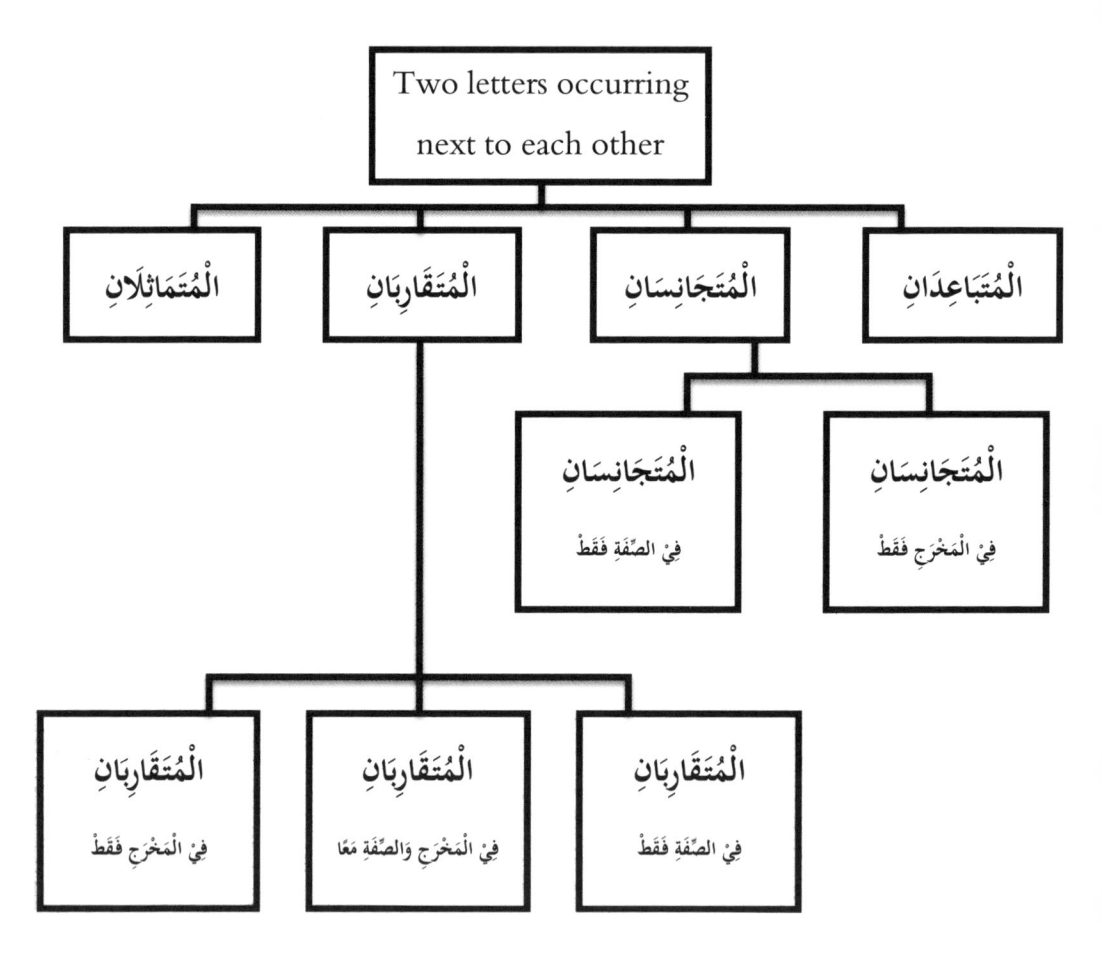

The following table defines and give an example for the seven situations:

| | Situation | Definition | Example |
|---|---|---|---|
| 1 | الْمُتَمَاثِلَانِ | These are those **two letters** that are **same** in the 'place of pronunciation' and **all** the 'qualities'. | فَقَالَ لَهُمْ |
| 2 | الْمُتَقَارِبَانِ فِيْ الْمَخْرَجِ وَالصِّفَةِ مَعًا | These are those **two letters** that are **close** to each other in the 'place of pronunciation' and the 'qualities'. | قُلْ رَبِّ |
| 3 | الْمُتَقَارِبَانِ فِيْ الْمَخْرَجِ فَقَطْ | These are those **two letters** that are **close** to each other in the 'place of pronunciation' only. | قَدْ سَمِعَ |
| 4 | الْمُتَقَارِبَانِ فِيْ الصِّفَةِ فَقَطْ | These are those **two letters** that are **close** to each other in 'qualities' only. | بِأَرْبَعَةِ شُهَدَاءِ |
| 5 | الْمُتَجَانِسَانِ فِيْ الْمَخْرَجِ فَقَطْ | These are those **two letters** that are the **same** in the 'place of pronunciation' only. | قَدْ تَبَيَّنَ |
| 6 | الْمُتَجَانِسَانِ فِيْ الصِّفَةِ فَقَطْ | These are those **two letters** that are the **same** in the 'qualities' only. | قَدْ جَعَلَ |
| 7 | الْمُتَبَاعِدَانِ | These are those **two letters** that are **different** in both; 'place of pronunciation' and **all** the 'qualities'. | أَنْعَمْتَ عَلَيْهِمْ |

<u>**Note**</u>: The 'qualities' of the letters are regarded **close** to each other only if **more than half** the 'qualities' are the **same**.

## Letters occurring next to each other in terms of *Harakah*

There are **three possible** situations for **two** letters occurring next to each other in terms of *harakah*:

1. Both the letters have a *harakah* – this is called الإِدْغَام الْكَبِيْر.
2. The first letter has a *saakin* and the second letter has a *harakah* – this is called الإِدْغَام الصَّغِيْر.
3. The first letter has a *harakah* and the second letter has a *saakin* – this is called الإِدْغَام الْمُطْلَق.

The table defines the three situations and mentions examples:

| | Situation | Definition | Example |
|---|---|---|---|
| 1 | الإِدْغَام الْكَبِيْر | When **both** the letters have a *harakah*. | الْكِتَاب |
| 2 | الإِدْغَام الصَّغِيْر | When the first letter has a *saakin* and the second letter has a *harakah*. | أَنْعَمْتَ |
| 3 | الإِدْغَام الْمُطْلَق | When the first letter has a *harakah* and the second letter has a *saakin*. | يُؤْمِنُوْنَ |

**Notes**:

(1) Logically there were four situations, however one situation has not been mentioned; namely, the two letters are *saakin*. The reason for omitting this situation is that **two *saakins* never occur next to each other in the Arabic language** except with certain conditions which will be discussed later.

(2) It is important to understand that these three terms do not have any individual rulings; instead the terms just need to be understood at this point. They will be used later with certain other rules.

(3) When these **three** situations of 'two letters occurring next to each other in terms of *harakah*' are multiplied with the **four** situations of 'two letters occurring next to each other in terms of pronunciation & 'qualities'; a total of **twelve** different situations occur.

### Twelve different situations for two letters occurring next to each other

As discussed, whenever two letters occur next to each other, there are 12 different possible situations when considering the 'place of pronunciation' of the letters, the 'qualities' of the letters and the *harakah* of the letters. However, the ruling of the twelve situations can differ in terms of *idghaam* & *izhaar*.

The table mentions the rulings and gives an example of the twelve situations:

|   | Situation |   | Will there be *Idghaam*? |   | Example |
|---|---|---|---|---|---|
| 1 |  | الْكَبِيْر | ✗ | Detail discussed below | فِيْهِ هُدًى |
| 2 | الْمُتَمَاثِلَانِ | الصَّغِيْر | ✓ | Detail discussed below | وَقَدْ دَّخَلُوْا |
| 3 |  | الْمُطْلَق | ✗ |  | شَقَقْنَا |
| 4 |  | الْكَبِيْر | ✗ | Detail discussed below | عَدَدَ سِنِيْنَ |
| 5 | الْمُتَقَارِبَانِ | الصَّغِيْر | ✗ | Detail discussed below | قَدْ سَمِعَ |
| 6 |  | الْمُطْلَق | ✗ |  | سِدْرَة |
| 7 |  | الْكَبِيْر | ✗ | Detail discussed below | الصَّالِحَاتِ طُوْبَى |
| 8 | الْمُتَجَانِسَانِ | الصَّغِيْر | ✗ | Detail discussed below | قَدْ جَعَلَ |
| 9 |  | الْمُطْلَق | ✗ |  | أَفَتَطْمَعُوْنَ |
| 10 |  | الْكَبِيْر | ✗ |  | أَنْعَمْتَ عَلَيْهِمْ |
| 11 | الْمُتَبَاعِدَانِ | الصَّغِيْر | ✗ |  | تُلِيَتْ عَلَيْهِمْ |
| 12 |  | الْمُطْلَق | ✗ |  | تَعْلَمُوْنَ |

**Note**: Six of the situations have further details which are discussed below.

First situation: ( الكبير ) ( المتماثلان )

When the two letters are الْمُتَمَاثِلَانِ (same letter) and الْكَبِيْر (both have a *harakah*) then **all the scholars except Imam *Susi*** mention there will be *izhaar;* meaning both letters will be prayed separately. Only Imam *Susi* (who is a transmitter from one of the seven famous *Qari's* (reciters), *Abu Amre al-Basri)* recites this situation with *idghaam*.

Example for the first situation: In the phrase [2:البقرة], فِيْهِ هُدًى , all the scholars pray the **two** (ه) separately, however, Imam *Susi* will join them together completely and pray (فِيْهُ هُدًى).

Second situation: ( الصغير ) ( المتماثلان )

When the two letters are الْمُتَمَاثِلَانِ (same letter) and الصَّغِيْر (first letter has a *saakin* and the second letter has a *harakah)* then **all the scholars** mention there will be *idghaam*. This *idghaam* is called الْإِدْغَام الصَّغِيْر. However, there are **two exceptions** to this rule;

- If the **first letter** is a letter of *madd* then there will be *izhaar* according to **all the scholars**; not *idghaam*. This is because the 'quality' of *madd* will be preserved within the first letter.
- If the **first letter** is هَاءُ السَّكْت then it is optional to do either; *idghaam* or *izhaar*, however, *izhaar* is the preferred opinion.

Example for the second situation: In the phrase [61:المائدة] وَقَدْ دَّخَلُوْا , all the scholars pray the **two** (د) merged, the first letter is merged into the second letter.

**Examples of exceptional cases**:

Example of the first letter being the letter of *madd:* In the phrase [82:البقرة] آمَنُوْا وَعَمِلُوا , despite **two same** letters (و) occurring together, there will **not** be *idghaam;* instead there will be *izhaar* as the first letter is from amongst the letters of *madd* .

**Note**: There are three letters of *madd* . They are:
- *waaw saakin* with a *dhammah* on the letter before, e.g. آمَنُوْا .
- *yaa saakin* with a *kasrah* on the letter before, e.g. فِيْ يَوْم .
- *alif saakin* with a *fathah* on the letter before, e.g. قَالَ .

Example of the first letter being the letter هَاءُ السَّكْت: In the phrase [28-29:الحاقة] ﴿28﴾ هَلَكَ مَالِيَهْ , despite **two same** letters (ه) occurring together, it will **not be necessary** to do *idghaam* when joining, instead it is optional to do *idghaam* or *izhaar; izhaar* being the preferred option.

**Note**: The term هَاءُ السَّكْت refers to such a *haa* which is **added on to certain words when stopping upon them**. There are rules when this *haa* can be added or not; this can be researched in grammer books. In the example given above the *idghaam* situation will be prayed as مَالِيَهَّلَكَ and the *izhaar* situation will be prayed as مَالِيَهْ هَلَكَ with a **small pause between the two letters, *haa*, without breathing**. If the reciter pauses and breaths between the two letters; they will be regarded as 'not occurring next to each other'; hence, this discussion will not apply.

Fourth situation: ( الْمُتَقَارِبَان ) ( الْكَبِيرُ )

When the two letters are الْمُتَقَارِبَان (close letter) and الْكَبِيرُ (both have a *harakah*) then **all the scholars except Imam *Susi*** mention there will be *izhaar;* meaning both letters will be prayed separately. Only Imam *Susi* recites this situation with *idghaam*.

Example for the fourth situation: In the phrase [المؤمنون:112] عَدَدَ سِنِيْنَ , all the scholars pray the first letter (د) and the second letter (س) separately; however, Imam *susi* will join them together completely and pray (عَدَدَ سِّنِيْنَ).

Fifth situation: ( الْمُتَقَارِبَان ) ( الصَّغِيرُ )

When the two letters are الْمُتَقَارِبَان (close letter) and الصَّغِيرُ (first letter has a *saakin* and the second letter has a *harakah*) then **many scholars** (including *Hafs al-Asadi*) mention there will be *izhaar*. However, there are **two exceptions** to this rule;

- If the **first letter** is the letter (ل) and the **second letter** is the letter (ر) , there will *idghaam*.
- If the **first letter** is the letter (ق) and the **second letter** is the letter (ك) , there will *idghaam*.

Example for the fifth situation: In the phrase [المجادلة:1] قَدْ سَمِعَ , all the scholars pray the first letter (د) and the second letter (س) separately.

**Examples of exceptional cases**:

Example of the first letter being (ل) and the second letter being (ر): In the phrase [طه:114] قُلْ رَّبِّ , the first letter (ل) will be merged into the second letter (ر); *idghaam* will occur.

Note: In the phrase [المطففين:14] بَلْ رَانَ , despite the letter (ل) occurring before the letter (ر); there will not be *idghaam* as according to Imam *Hafs*, *sakt* will occur here. The discussion of *sakt* will be mentioned later.

Example of the first letter being (ق) and the second letter being (ك): In the phrase [المرسلات:20] أَلَمْ نَخْلُقْكُمْ , the first letter (ق) will be merged into the second letter (ك); *idghaam* will occur.

Note: Scholars have differed whether there will be 'complete *idghaam*' or 'incomplete *idghaam*' when the (ق) is merged with (ك); some say the 'quality' of استعلاء will remain in the (ق). **The correct view is that there will be 'complete *idghaam*'**.

Seventh situation: ( الكبير ) ( المتجانسان )

When the two letters are الْمُتَجَانِسَان (letters are same in either مخرج or صفات) and الْكَبِير (both have a *harakah*) then **all the scholars except Imam *Susi*** mention there will be *izhaar;* meaning both letters will be prayed separately. Only Imam *Susi* recites this situation with *idghaam*.

Example for the seventh situation: In the phrase [29:الرعد] الصَّالِحَاتِ طُوبَى , all the scholars pray the first letter (ت) and the second letter (ط) separately; however, Imam *Susi* will join them together completely and pray (الصَّالِحَاتُ طُوبَى).

Eighth situation: ( الصغير ) ( المتجانسان )

When the two letters are الْمُتَجَانِسَان (letters are same in either مخرج or صفات) and الصَّغِير (first letter has a *saakin* and the second letter has a *harakah*) then **many scholars** (including *Hafs al-Asadi*) mention there will be *izhaar*. However, there are **seven exceptions** to this rule.

Example for the eighth situation: In the phrase [24:مريم] قَدْ جَعَلَ , all the scholars pray the first letter (د) and the second letter (ج) separately.

The **seven exceptions** to this rule are;

- If the **first letter** is the letter (ت) and the **second letter** is the letter (د) there will *idghaam*.
  Example: In the phrase [89:يونس] أُجِيبَتْ دَعْوَتُكُمَا , there will *idghaam*.
- If the **first letter** is the letter (د) and the **second letter** is the letter (ت) there will *idghaam*.
  Example: In the phrase [256:البقرة] قَدْ تَبَيَّنَ , there will *idghaam*.
- If the **first letter** is the letter (ت) and the **second letter** is the letter (ط) there will *idghaam*.
  Example: In the phrase [72:آل عمران] قَالَتْ طَائِفَةٌ , there will *idghaam*.
- If the **first letter** is the letter (ط) and the **second letter** is the letter (ت) there will *idghaam*.
  Example: In the phrase [28:المائدة] بَسَطْتَ , there will *idghaam*.
- If the **first letter** is the letter (ث) and the **second letter** is the letter (ذ) there will *idghaam*.
  Example: In the phrase [176:آل عمران] يَلْهَثْ ذَٰلِكَ , there will *idghaam*.
- If the **first letter** is the letter (ذ) and the **second letter** is the letter (ظ) there will *idghaam*.
  Example: In the phrase [64:النساء] إِذْ ظَلَمُوا , there will *idghaam*.
- If the **first letter** is the letter (ب) and the **second letter** is the letter (م) there will *idghaam*.
  Example: In the phrase [42:هود] ارْكَبْ مَعَنَا , there will *idghaam*.

**Note**: In all seven exceptions there will be 'complete *idghaam*' **except** for the case where the letter (ط) is being merged into the letter (ت); it will be 'incomplete *idghaam*' as the '**quality**' of إطباق which is possessed in the letter (ط) will remain.

## In brief:

Below the **twelve situations** are mentioned very briefly as a recap and for easy memorisation:

- **All** the الْمُطْلَق situations (total of 4 situations) will be performed with *izhaar* according to **all scholars, without any exceptions**.

- **All** the الْمُتَبَاعِدَان situations (total of 3 situations) will be performed with *izhaar* according to **all scholars without any exceptions**.

- **All** the الْكَبِيْر situations **except** the (الْمُتَبَاعِدَان الْكَبِيْر) (total of 3 situations) will be performed with *izhaar* according to **all scholars except Imam Susi**, he does الإدغام الكبير in them.

- In the situation (الْمُتَمَاثِلَانِ الصَّغِيْر) **all the scholars will do *idghaam*, which is called** الإدغام الصّغير.

- In the situation (الْمُتَقَارِبَانِ الصَّغِيْر) **many scholars** (including *Hafs al-Asadi*) will do *izhaar* **except in two letters**.

- In the situation (الْمُتَجَانِسَانِ الصَّغِيْر) **many scholars** (including *Hafs al-Asadi*) will do *izhaar* **except in seven letters**.

Additional rules:

There are some additional rules which are mentioned before the completion of this chapter. These rules are:

- When *idghaam* occurs a *tashdeed* will appear on the second letter, resulting in doubling the length of pronunciation of this letter. Example: وَقَدْ دَّخَلُوا [المجادلة:61] .

- When (ال) appears before certain **fourteen** letters of the alphabet, there will be *izhaar*. These letters are:

  ( اِبْغِ حَجَّكَ وَخِفْ عَقِيْمَهُ )

  These fourteen letters are called الْحُرُوْف الْقَمْرِيَّة (the lunar letters).

- When (ال) appears before certain **fourteen** letters of the alphabet, there will be *idghaam*. These letters are:

  ( سَتَرِدُّ ضَلَّ نَظَرٍ صَنْطِ شَذٍ )

  These fourteen letters are called الْحُرُوْف الشَّمْسِيَّة (the solar letters).

- The six letters from الْحُرُوْف الْحَلْقِيَّة will **never merge** with any letter except itself. Only if the letter is repeated then it will merge with the same letter.

- All the rules mentioned in the chapter of *idghaam* will only apply when the two letters focussed upon are prayed together; if one of the letters is occurring at the end of the first word and the second letter is occurring at the beginning of the second word and the reciter pauses between the two words, there will **not be idghaam**. *Idghaam* only applies in the state of continued recitation between the two letters focussed upon.

Example: In the phrase مَالِيَهْ ﴿28﴾ هَلَكَ [الحاقة:28-29], despite there being two same letters (ه) appearing together, if the reciter decides to stop on the first (ه) there will be no *idghaam*, as the two letters are separated by the pausing.

# Rules of the pronoun (ه)

## Definition of the pronoun (ه)

The pronoun (ه) indicates upon **singular, masculine and 3<sup>rd</sup> person** (واحد مذكّر غائب).

## Rules of the pronoun (ه)

The *harakah* occurring on the pronoun (ه) will be either *kasrah* ( ِ ), *dhammah* ( ُ ), or *sukoon* ( ْ ). The following rules mention which *harakah* will be recited upon the pronoun (ه):

- If before the pronoun (ه) there is a *kasrah* or *yaa saakin* the *harakah* upon the pronoun (ه) will be a *kasrah*.

    Example: In the word بِهِ the pronoun (ه) will be recited with a *kasrah* due to the *kasrah* occurring before it.

    In the word إِلَيْهِ the pronoun (ه) will be recited with a *kasrah* due to the *yaa saakin* occurring before it.

- If before the pronoun (ه) there is anything other than a *kasrah* or *yaa saakin* then the *harakah* upon the pronoun (ه) will be a *dhammah*.

    Example: In the word لَهُ the pronoun (ه) will be recited with a *dhammah* due to the *fathah* before it.

    In the word مِنْهُ the pronoun (ه) will be recited with a *dhammah* due to the *saakin* before it.

- In the state of pausing upon the pronoun (ه) it will be recited with a *saakin*.

    Example: In the word إِلَيْهِ the pronoun (ه) will be recited with a *saakin* due to pausing.

**Notes**: There are some exceptions to the rules mentioned above. These are indicated below:

- According to Imam *Hafs*, in **two places** within the Qur'an the pronoun (ه) will be recited with a *dhammah* despite having a *yaa saakin* before it. The two places are:
    1. وَمَا أَنسَانِيهُ [الكهف:63]
    2. عَلَيْهُ اللَّهَ [الفتح:10]

- According to Imam *Hafs*, in **two places** within the Qur'an the pronoun (ه) will be recited with a *saakin* despite having a *kasrah* before it. The two places are:
    1. أَرْجِهْ [الأعراف:111]
    2. فَأَلْقِهْ [النمل:28]

- According to Imam *Hafs*, in **one place** within the Qur'an the pronoun (ه) will be recited with a *kasrah* despite having a *saakin* before it. This place is:
    1. وَيَتَّقْهِ فَأُولَٰئِكَ [النور:52]

# Rules of the pronoun (هـ) and صلة

There are certain rules of the pronoun (هـ) in terms of صلة.

## Definition of الصِّلَة

This is to stretch the *dhammah* to such an extent that the letter *waaw* is pronounced **after it**, or to stretch the *kasrah* to such an extent that the letter *yaa* is pronounced **after it**.

## Rules of the pronoun (هـ) in terms of صلة

The pronoun (هـ) has the following rules in terms of صلة:
- If the pronoun (هـ) is between **two *mutaharrik*** letters, صِلَة will occur.
- If the pronoun (هـ) has a *saakin* **before**, **after** or on **both sides**, صِلَة will **not** occur.

The following table gives an example of few situations and mentions whether صلة will occur or not:

| | Example | Will صلة occur? | Explanation |
|---|---|---|---|
| 1 | إِنَّهُ هُوَ | ✓ | There is a **harakah on both sides** of the pronoun (هـ), hence صلة **will** occur. |
| 2 | فِيهِ هُدًى | ✗ | There is a *saakin* **before** the pronoun (هـ), hence صلة will **not** occur. |
| 3 | إِنَّهُ الْحَقُّ | ✗ | There is a *saakin* **after** the pronoun (هـ), hence صلة will **not** occur. |
| 4 | مِنْهُ الْمَاءَ | ✗ | There is a *saakin* on **both sides** of the pronoun (هـ), hence صلة will **not** occur. |

**Notes**: There are some exceptions to the rules mentioned above. These are indicated below:
- According to Imam *Hafs*, in **two places** within the Qur'an the pronoun (هـ) will be prayed against the normal rules of صلة. The two places are:
    1. وَمَا أَنْسَانِيهُ [الكهف:63]
    2. عَلَيْهُ الله [الفتح:10]
- In the phrase وَإِن تَشْكُرُوا يَرْضَهُ لَكُمْ [الزمر:7], despite a *harakah* occurring on **both sides** of the pronoun (هـ) there will **not be** صِلَة as the original wording was يَرْضَاهُ لَكُمْ ; a *saakin* before the pronoun (هـ).
- In the phrase فِيهِ مُهَانًا [الفرقان:69] despite *saakin* occurring **before** the pronoun (هـ) there **will be** صِلَة.
- Whenever a 'plural *meem*' occurs before an **attached pronoun**; a *waaw* will be added in writing and in pronunciation between the 'plural *meem*' and the **attached pronoun**. This will create a صِلَة.
Example: The word طَلَّقْتُمُوهُنَّ [البقرة:237] was originally طَلَّقْتُمْ with a 'plural *meem*' at the end, as the following was the attached pronoun ( هُنَّ ), the letter *waaw* was inserted inbetween.

# Types & Rules of *Madd*

The different types of *madd* will be defined below with any important notes; thereafter the rulings for will be mentioned.

## Definition of *Madd*

| | Type | Definition |
|---|---|---|
| 1 | المدّ<br>*Madd* | This is to **stretch** & **lengthen** the voice due to one of the letters of *madd* occurring. |

## Letters of *Madd*

There are **three** letters of *madd*. They are:

1. *alif* (ا) with a *fathah* **before** it.
2. *waaw saakin* (وْ) with a *dhammah* **before** it.
3. *yaa saakin* (يْ) with a *kasrah* **before** it.

**Notes**:

(1) The letter *alif* **does not** have any *harakah* upon it, if any *harakah* does appear on this letter then this letter will be regarded as a *hamzah*, not an *alif*.

(2) The *harakah* on the letter before the *alif* will **always** be *fathah*. Therefore, the letter *alif* will **always** be regarded as one of the letters of *madd*.

(3) Some scholars have given the example of [هود:49] نُوحِيهَا , for gathering all three different types of *madd*.

(4) It is important for the *waaw* and *yaa* to have a *saakin* upon them if they are to be regarded as a letter of *madd*; otherwise they will not be regarded as a letter of *madd*.

(5) If the letters *waaw* or *yaa* have a *saakin* upon it, and the *harakah* prior to them is a **fathah** then the *waaw* or *yaa* will be regarded as the letters of *leen* (لَيْن).

Examples:

- In the word [قريش:4] خَوْف , there is a *waaw saakin* with a *fathah* **before** it, hence the *waaw saakin* will be regarded as a letter of *leen*.
- In the word [البقرة:2] رَيْب , there is a *yaa saakin* with a *fathah* **before** it, hence the *yaa saakin* will be regarded as a letter of *leen*.

## Types of *Madd*

There are two types of *madd*:

- المدّ الأصلي (المدّ الطبيعي) – an original (natural) *madd*
- المدّ الفرعي – derived *madd*

The table below defines the two types of *madd* and gives examples for each:

|   | Term | Definition | Example |
|---|------|------------|---------|
| 1 | الأصلي | **Dictionary**: 'original' <br> **Terminology**: This is the type of *madd* where the **stretching** of the noise is **done** due to the letters of *madd* themselves; not because of any external reason (a *hamzah* or a *saakin* occurring after one of the letters of *madd*). | مَالِك <br> كَثِيرَة <br> مَرْفُوعَة |
| 2 | الفرعي | **Dictionary**: 'subsidiary' or 'secondary' <br> **Terminology**: This is the type of *madd* where the **stretching** of the noise is **not done** due to the letters of *madd* themselves; instead the stretch is done due to a *hamzah* or *saakin* coming after one of the letters of *madd*. | السَّمَاء <br> بِمَا أُنْزِلَ <br> آمَنُوا |

**Notes**:

(1) المدّ الأصلي is also called المدّ الطبيعي (the 'natural' *madd*), as the reciters who have a 'natural' sense of the Arabic language will **stretch** these letters according to its correct length, without increasing or decreasing it.

(2) There are two **secondary reasons** for *madd* to occur:
- A *hamzah* occurring after one of the letters of *madd*.
- A *saakin* occurring after one of the letters of *madd*.

## Types of المدّ الأصلي (المدّ الطبيعي) – original *madd*:

There are **two** types of 'original *madd*':

- المدّ الأصلي الكِلْمي
- المدّ الأصلي الحَرْفي

The table below defines the two types of 'original *madd*' and gives examples for each:

|   | Term | Definition | Example |
|---|------|------------|---------|
| 1 | الكلمي | **Dictionary**: 'word' <br> **Terminology**: This is such a type of 'original *madd*' where one of the letters of *madd* is present clearly **in the word**. | مَالِك <br> كَثِيْرَة <br> مَرْفُوْعَة |
| 2 | الحرفي | **Dictionary**: 'letter' <br> **Terminology**: This is such a type of 'original *madd*' where one of the letters of *madd* is **not** present in the word, instead it is only present when reciting certain **letters**. | حٰم <br> كهيعص <br> طٰسٓمٓ |

**Note**:

المدّ الأصلي الحرفي is only present at the beginning of some chapters of the Qur'an. This type of المدّ الأصلي only occurs with **five** letters which are gathered in the mnemonic "حَيْ طَهَرَ".

The table below mentions all the different words in the Qur'an where المدّ الأصلي الحرفي occurs:

|   | Letter | Example |
|---|--------|---------|
| 1 | ح | حٰم [سورة غافر وفصّلت والشورى والزخرف والدخان والجاثية والأحقاف] <br> This letter occurs at the beginning of **seven** chapters (as mentioned). |
| 2 | ي | كهيعص [سورة مريم] ، يٰس [سورة يس] <br> This letter occurs at the beginning of **two** chapters (as mentioned). |
| 3 | ط | طٰه [سورة طه] ، طٰسٓمٓ [سورة الشعراء والقصص] ، طٰسٓ [سورة النمل] <br> This letter occurs at the beginning of **four** chapters (as mentioned). |
| 4 | ه | كهيعص [سورة مريم] ، طٰه [سورة طه] <br> This letter occurs at the beginning of **two** chapters (as mentioned). |
| 5 | ر | الٓر [سورة يونس وهود ويوسف وإبراهيم والحجر] ، الٓمٓر [سورة الرعد] <br> This letter occurs at the beginning of **six** chapters (as mentioned). |

**Notes**:

(1) In total there are **ten** words, **twenty-one** letters within the Qur'an where المدّ الأصلي الحرفي takes place.

(2) These **twenty-one** letters are regarded from المدّ الأصلي because the **second letter** pronounced when praying these letters is one of the letters of *madd* and there is no *saakin* or *hamzah* after them, hence المدّ الأصلي.

Example: In the example [1:يونس الٓر], the letter (ر) is regarded as المدّ الأصلي الحرفي because when reciting this letter, *alif* is pronounced after the *raa*, (ر) without a *saakin* or *hamzah* occurring after the *alif*.

## Types of المدّ الفرعي – derived *Madd*:

There are **five** types of 'derived *madd*':

- المدّ الفرعي المتّصل
- المدّ الفرعي المنفصل
- المدّ الفرعي البدل
- المدّ الفرعي العارض
- المدّ الفرعي اللازم

The table below defines the five types of 'derived *madd*' and gives examples for each:

| | Term | Definition | Example |
|---|---|---|---|
| 1 | المتّصل | **Dictionary**: 'joint' <br> **Terminology**: This is such a type of 'derived *madd*' where a *hamzah* is present **directly after** one of the letters of *madd* in the **same** word. | السَّمَاء <br> النَّسِيْءُ <br> قُرُوْءُ |
| 2 | المنفصل | **Dictionary**: 'separate' <br> **Terminology**: This is such a type of 'derived *madd*' where a *hamzah* is present **directly after** one of the letters of *madd*, in the following (separate) word. | بِمَا أُنْزِلَ <br> قَالُوا آمَنَّا <br> ارْجِعِيْ إِلَى رَبِّكِ |
| 3 | البدل | **Dictionary**: 'change' <br> **Terminology**: This is such a type of 'derived *madd*' where **two** *hamzah's* appear together in one word, in this case the second *hamzah* will be changed to a letter of *madd* according to the *harakah* of the letter before. | آمَنُوا <br> إِيْمَانًا <br> أُوْتِيَ |
| 4 | العارض | **Dictionary**: 'temporary' <br> **Terminology**: This is such a type of 'derived *madd*' where a **temporary** *saakin* is present **directly after** one of the letters of *madd*. | الْبَيَانْ <br> نَسْتَعِيْنْ <br> الْمُفْلِحُوْنْ |
| 5 | اللّازم | **Dictionary**: 'compulsory' or 'permanently' <br> **Terminology**: This is such a type of 'derived *madd*' where a **permanent** *saakin* is present **directly after** one of the letters of *madd*. | دَابَّة <br> آلْآنَ <br> أَلَمْ |

**Notes**:

(1) In المدّ الفرعي البدل when **two** *hamzah's* appear together and the second *hamzah* is changed to a letter of *madd*; this changing is called **ibdaal**.

(2) In المدّ الفرعي العارض the **temporary** *saakin* is created by **stopping or pausing** upon a word.

Types of المدّ الفرعي المتّصل :

There are **two** types of المدّ الفرعي المتّصل :

- المدّ الفرعي المتّصل **المتطرّف**
- المدّ الفرعي المتّصل **المتوسّط**

The table below defines the two types of المدّ الفرعي المتّصل and gives examples for each:

| | Term | Definition | Example |
|---|---|---|---|
| 1 | المتطرّف | **Dictionary**: 'edge' <br> **Terminology**: This is such a type of المدّ الفرعي المتّصل where the *hamzah* which is occurring directly after the letter of *madd* is at the **end** of the word. | السَّمَاء <br> نَسِيْءٌ <br> قُرُوْءٌ |
| 2 | المتوسّط | **Dictionary**: 'inbetween' <br> **Terminology**: This is such a type of المدّ الفرعي المتّصل where the *hamzah* which is occurring directly after the letter of *madd* is **inbetween** the word. | إِسْرَائِيل <br> أَشْيَاءَهُم <br> الأَرَائِك |

**Note**: The ruling of المدّ الفرعي المتّصل المتطرّف and المدّ الفرعي المتّصل المتوسّط is the same when the recitation is continued, however when **pausing or stopping**; the rules of *madd* will differ slightly. (The rules of *madd* will be discussed shortly).

Types of المدّ الفرعي اللازم :

There are **four** types of المدّ الفرعي اللازم :

- المدّ الفرعي اللازم **الكلمي المثقّل**
- المدّ الفرعي اللازم **الكلمي المخفّف**
- المدّ الفرعي اللازم **الحرفي المثقّل**
- المدّ الفرعي اللازم **الحرفي المخفّف**

The table below defines the four types of المدّ الفرعي المتّصل and gives examples for each:

|   | Term | Definition | Example |
|---|------|------------|---------|
| 1 | الكلمي المثقّل | This is such a type of المدّ الفرعي اللازم where the *saakin* is present in a **word** which **has** a *tashdeed* upon it due to *idghaam*. | دَابَّة أَتُحَاجُّونِّي |
| 2 | الكلمي المخفّف | This is such a type of المدّ الفرعي اللازم where the *saakin* is present in a **word** which **does not** have a *tashdeed* upon it. | آلْآنَ |
| 3 | الحرفي المثقّل | This is such a type of المدّ الفرعي اللازم where the *saakin* is present in a **letter** which **has** a *tashdeed* upon it due to *idghaam*. | الٓمٓ طسٓمٓ |
| 4 | الحرفي المخفّف | This is such a type of المدّ الفرعي اللازم where the *saakin* is present in a **letter** which **does not** have a *tashdeed* upon it. | الٓر قٓ |

**Notes**:

(1) المدّ الفرعي اللازم الكلمي المخفّف only occurs in **one** word within the Qur'an.

The word آلْآنَ which occurs **twice**:

- آلْآنَ وَقَدْ كُنْتُمْ بِهِ تَسْتَعْجِلُونَ [يونس:51]
- آلْآنَ وَقَدْ عَصَيْتَ قَبْلُ وَكُنْتَ مِنَ الْمُفْسِدِينَ [يونس:91]

(2) المدّ الفرعي اللازم الحرفي is only present at the beginning of some chapters of the Qur'an. This type of المدّ الفرعي اللازم only occurs with **eight** letters which are gathered in the mnemonic "سَنَقُصُّ عِلْمَكَ".

The table below mentions all the different words in the Qur'an where المدّ الفرعي اللازم الحرفي occurs:

| | Letter | Example |
|---|---|---|
| 1 | س | طسٓمٓ [سورة الشعراء والقصص] ، طسٓ [سورة النمل] ، يسٓ [سورة يس] ، حمٓ عسٓقٓ [سورة الشورى]<br>This letter occurs at the beginning of **five** chapters. |
| 2 | ن | نٓ وَالْقَلَمِ [سورة القلم]<br>This letter occurs at the beginning of **one** chapter only. |
| 3 | ق | حمٓ عسٓقٓ [سورة الشورى] ، قٓ وَالْقُرْآنِ [سورة ق]<br>This letter occurs at the beginning of **two** chapters. |
| 4 | ص | المٓصٓ [سورة الأعراف] ، كهيعصٓ [سورة مريم] ، صٓ وَالْقُرْآنِ [سورة ص]<br>This letter occurs at the beginning of **three** chapters. |
| 5 | ع | كهيعصٓ [سورة مريم] ، حمٓ عسٓقٓ [سورة الشورى]<br>This letter occurs at the beginning of **two** chapters. |
| 6 | ل | الٓمٓ [سورة البقرة وآل عمران والعنكبوت والروم ولقمان والسجدة] ، الٓر [سورة يونس وهود ويوسف وإبراهيم والحجر] ، المٓصٓ [سورة الأعراف] ، الٓمٓر [سورة الرعد]<br>This letter occurs at the beginning of **thirteen** chapters. |
| 7 | م | الٓمٓ [سورة البقرة وآل عمران والعنكبوت والروم ولقمان والسجدة] ، المٓصٓ [سورة الأعراف] ، الٓمٓر [سورة الرعد] ، طسٓمٓ [سورة الشعراء والقصص] ، حمٓ [سورة غافر وفصّلت والشورى والزخرف والدخان والجاثية والأحقاف]<br>This letter occurs at the beginning of **seventeen** chapters. |
| 8 | ك | كهيعصٓ [سورة مريم]<br>This letter occurs at the beginning of **one** chapter only. |

**Notes**:

(1) In total there are **twenty-two** words, **forty-four** letters within the Qur'an where المدّ الفرعي الحرفي takes place.

(2) In all the words mentioned above for المدّ الفرعي الحرفي, it will be from the category of المخفّف **except with two words**; it will be المثقّل. They are:
- The (ل) in [1:البقرة] الٓمٓ , as there will be *idghaam* in the following letter, (م).
- The (س) in [1:الشعراء] طسٓمٓ , as there will be *idghaam* in the following letter, (م).

(3) In all **eight letters** mentioned above, according to **all** scholars the rules of المدّ الفرعي اللازم will apply **except** in the letter (ع). In this letter there is an option; the rules of المدّ الفرعي اللازم or the rules of لين can apply. **This applies to both the examples of** (ع).

From the tables above a total of **eleven** different types of *madd* are indicated. The following flowchart illustrates:

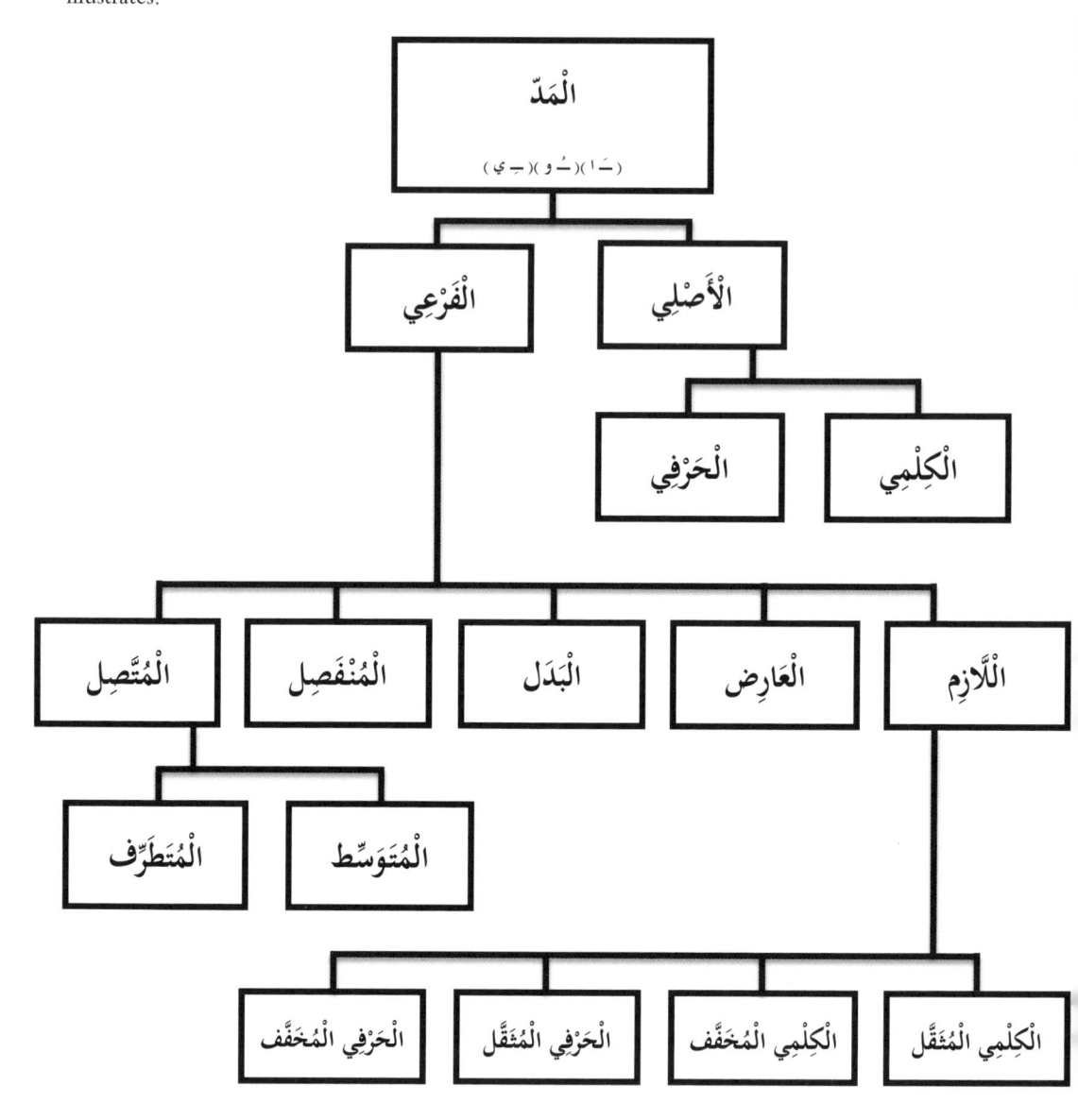

```
                          الْمَدّ
                      ( ـَ ا )( ـُ و )( ـِ ي )
                            │
              ┌─────────────┴─────────────┐
          الْفَرْعِي                      الْأَصْلِي
              │                            │
              │                    ┌───────┴───────┐
              │                 الْحَرْفِي      الْكِلْمِي
              │
   ┌──────┬───┴───┬──────┬──────┐
الْمُتَّصِل  الْمُنْفَصِل  الْبَدَل  الْعَارِض  اللَّازِم
    │                                  │
 ┌──┴──┐                               │
الْمُتَطَرِّف الْمُتَوَسِّط                     │
                                       │
                   ┌──────┬────────┬───┴────────┐
            الْحَرْفِي   الْحَرْفِي  الْكِلْمِي   الْكِلْمِي
            الْمُخَفَّف  الْمُثَقَّل  الْمُخَفَّف   الْمُثَقَّل
```

**Note**: In addition to the **eleven** different types of *madd* situations, there are also the letters of *leen* which were mentioned earlier. The situations of the letters of *leen* can be divided into **three categories**;

1. اللين
2. اللين اللازم
3. اللين العارض

Therefore, in total the rulings for **fourteen** situations will be mentioned in the table below after defining all the types.

The table below defines all fourteen different types of *madd* or *leen* and gives examples for each:

|  | Term | Definition | Example |
|---|---|---|---|
| 1 | المدّ الأصلي الكلمي | This is such a type of *madd* where the **stretching** is done due to a letter of *madd* itself (which is present in writing), **not** because of a *hamzah* or *saakin* coming after one of the letters of *madd*. | مَالِك<br>كَثِيْرَة<br>مَرْفُوْعَة |
| 2 | المدّ الأصلي الحرفي | This is such a type of *madd* where the **stretching** is done due to a letter of *madd* itself (which is not present in writing), **not** because of a *hamzah* or *saakin* coming after one of the letters of *madd*. | حٰم<br>كٓهيٰعٓصٓ<br>طٰسٓم |
| 3 | المدّ الفرعي المتصل المتوسّط | This is such a type of *madd* where *hamzah* occurs **directly after** the letter of *madd* in the **same** word, **inbetween** the word. | إِسْرَائِيْل<br>أَشْيَاءَهُم<br>الْأَرَائِك |
| 4 | المدّ الفرعي المتّصل المتطرّف | This is such a type of *madd* where *hamzah* occurs **directly after** the letter of *madd* in the **same** word at the **end** of the word. | السَّمَاء<br>نَسِيْء<br>قُرُوْء |
| 5 | المدّ الفرعي المنفصل | This is such a type of *madd* where *hamzah* occurs **directly after** the letter of *madd* in a **separate** (following) word. | بِمَا أُنْزِل<br>قَالُوْا آمَنَّا<br>ارْجِعِيْ إِلٰى رَبِّك |
| 6 | المدّ الفرعي البدل | This is such a type of *madd* where **two** *hamzah's* appear together in one word, in this case the second *hamzah* will be changed to a letter of *madd* according to the *harakah* of the first *hamzah*. | آمَنُوْا<br>إِيْمَانًا<br>أُوْتِي |
| 7 | المدّ الفرعي العارض | This is such a type of *madd* where **directly after** one of the letters of *madd*, a **temporary** *saakin* is present. | الْبَيَان<br>نَسْتَعِيْن<br>الْمُفْلِحُوْن |
| 8 | المدّ الفرعي اللّازم الكلميّ المثقّل | This is such a type of *madd* where **directly after** one of the letters of *madd*, a **permanent** *saakin* is present. This *saakin* is present in a **word** which has a *tashdeed* upon it due to *idghaam*. | دَابَّة<br>أَتُحَاجُّوْنِّي<br>الضَّالِّيْن |
| 9 | المدّ الفرعي اللّازم الكلميّ المخفّف | This is such a type of *madd* where **directly after** one of the letters of *madd*, a **permanent** *saakin* is present. This *saakin* is present in a **word** which **does not** have a *tashdeed* upon it. | آلْآن |
| 10 | المدّ الفرعي اللّازم الحرفي المثقّل | This is such a type of *madd* where **directly after** one of the letters of *madd*, a **permanent** *saakin* is present. This *saakin* is present in a **letter** which has a *tashdeed* upon it due to *idghaam*. | الٓمٓ<br>طٰسٓمٓ |

| | | | |
|---|---|---|---|
| 11 | المدّ الفرعي اللّازم الحرفي المخفّف | This is such a type of *madd* where **directly after** one of the letters of *madd*, a **permanent** *saakin* is present. This *saakin* is present in a **letter** which **does not** have a *tashdeed* upon it. | اَلَر<br>قَ |
| 12 | اللين | This is such a word which has a *waaw saakin* or *yaa saakin* present with a *fathah* before it. | خَوْفٌ<br>رَيْبٌ |
| 13 | اللين اللازم | This is such a word which has one of the letters of *leen* and has a **compulsory** *saakin* after it. Example: The letter ع in كهيعص or حم عسق | كهيعص<br>حم عسق |
| 14 | اللين العارض | This is such a word which has one of the letters of *leen* and has a **temporary** *saakin* after it. | خَوْفٌ<br>رَيْبٌ |

The table below mentions the rule of all the different types of *madd* or *leen*:

| | Term | Length of Madd/Leen | Rule | Reason | Example |
|---|---|---|---|---|---|
| 1 | المدّ الأصلي الكلمي | 2 Harakaat | Compulsory | All the scholars pray المدّ الأصلي with the normal length of praying one letter, (which is referred to as 2 *harakaat*). | مَالِك كَثِيرَة مَرْفُوعَة |
| 2 | المدّ الأصلي الحرفي | 2 Harakaat | Compulsory | | حم كهيعص طسم |
| 3 | المدّ الفرعي المتصل المتوسّط | 4-5 Harakaat | Compulsory | All the scholars have agreed to *madd* in المتصل situation. | إِسْرَائِيل أَشْيَاءَهُم الْأَرَائِك |
| 4 | المدّ الفرعي المتصل المتطرّف | 4-5 Harakaat | Compulsory | | السَّمَاء نَسِيْء قُرُوْء |
| 5 | المدّ الفرعي المنفصل | 4–5 Harakaat | Permissible | Some scholars have agreed to *madd* in المنفصل situation, others have not prayed *madd*; hence both are permissible, doing *madd* is preferred. | بِمَا أُنزِلَ قَالُوا آمَنَّا ارْجِعِي إِلَى رَبِّكِ |
| 6 | المدّ الفرعي البدل | 2 Harakaat | Compulsory | It is compulsory to change the second *hamzah* to an appropriate letter of *madd* according to most scholars of grammar. | آمَنُوا إِيمَانًا أُوتِي |
| 7 | المدّ الفرعي العارض | 2, 4 or 6 Harakaat | Permissible | All the scholars have given an option in praying with or without *madd* in العارض situation. | الْبَيَان نَسْتَعِين الْمُفْلِحُون |
| 8 | المدّ الفرعي اللازم الكلميّ المثقل | 6 Harakaat | Compulsory | All the scholars have agreed to *madd* in اللازم situation. | دَابَّة أَتُحَاجُّونِّي الضَّالِّين |
| 9 | المدّ الفرعي اللازم الكلميّ المخفف | | | | آلْآن |
| 10 | المدّ الفرعي اللازم الحرفي المثقل | | | | الم طسم |
| 11 | المدّ الفرعي اللازم الحرفي المخفف | | | | الر ق |

| 12 | اللين | 2, 4 or 6 *Harakaat* | Permissible | According to **all** scholars it is permissible to stretch the letter from 2-6 *harakaat* in this situation. It is generally preferred to shorten the *leen* length. | خَوْفٌ<br>زَيْبٌ |
|---|---|---|---|---|---|
| 13 | اللين اللازم | | | | كهيعص<br>حم عسق |
| 14 | اللين العارض | | | | خَوْفٌ<br>زَيْبٌ |

**Notes**:

(1) It is very important to understand that there is a great debate amongst scholars regarding the different lengths of *madd*, hence many books will indicate to slightly different lengths. In the table above the lowest lengths are used.

(2) The lengths of the *madd* mentioned above are in terms of *harakaat*, however many books mention the lengths in terms of *alif* (or letters). The key is that the length of **one letter** is equivalent to **two** *harakaat*. Therefore, المدّ الأصلي which is **two** *harakaat* will be equivalent of **one letter** (or one *alif*).

(3) Some books have referred to the lengths of the *madd* as قَصْر , تَوَسُّط & طُوْل.

The length of قَصْر is **two** *harakaat* (**one letter**).

The length of تَوَسُّط is **four** *harakaat* (**two letters**), to **six** *harakaat* (**three letters**).

The length of طُوْل is **six** *harakaat* (**three letters**), to **ten** *harakaat* (**five letters**).

(4) Scholars have differed in the length of طُوْل and تَوَسُّط as mentioned above. As mentioned it is permissible to adopt any view. **However, it is not permissible to keep changing the view within one recitation.**

**Example**: If the length of طُوْل is adopted as **six** *harakaat* in the recitation, then for the remainder of that recitation **six** *harakaat* will be practiced for طُوْل. It is **not permissible** to change it to **ten** *harakaat*.

(5) In المدّ المتّصل and المدّ المنفصل the length of Madd is 4-5 *harakaat*; however, it is important to note that the **same** length should be adopted for both or المدّ المتّصل is given preference.

(6) In المدّ الفرعي العارض and اللين العارض it is permissible to stretch the letter for the length of 2, 4 or 6 *harakaat*. However, the difference between the two is that in المدّ الفرعي العارض it is better to pray 6 *harakaat*, then 4 and then 2 – it is better to lengthen the *madd*. On the other hand, in اللين العارض it is better to do 2 *harakaat*, then 4 and then 6 – it is better to shorten the *leen*.

(7) From amongst the **four** types of المدّ الفرعي اللازم mentioned above, according to **most** scholars the length of all **four types** will be the same – 6 *harakaat*. However, according to **some scholars** the stretching in the مثقّل types will be more than the مخفّف types.

(8) In some of the types of *madd* and *leen* mentioned above there were different lengths permissible when stretching. However, it is **not permissible** to do الخَلْط في الرِّوايات according to scholars. This means that it is **not permissible** to change the length of a certain *madd* or *leen* in one recitation.

**Example**: If the reciter is reading and for the first المدّ العارض the reciter decides to pray the length of **two harakaat**, then it is compulsory upon the reciter to recite المدّ العارض with the duration of **two harakaat** whenever it occurs in that specific recitation.

(9) The length of stretching in *madd* is given priority over the length of stretching in *leen* as the quality of stretching is **originally** for *madd* and **secondary** in *leen*. Therefore, in one verse of the Qur'an if المدّ العارض and

اللين العارض gather then according to the lengths mentioned above it is permissible to stretch upto 2,4 or 6 *harakaat* in each type. However, if the reciter chooses to pray المدّ العارض with 4 *harakaat* length then it is **not permissible** to recite اللين العارض with 6 *harakaat* as the 'quality' of stretching is weaker in *leen*. Therefore, it is permissible to pray with 4 or 2 *harakaat*. (More detail of this will be mentioned later).

(10) If after one of the letters of *madd* a *saakin* appears in the next word then the letters of *madd* will be dropped in pronunciation when joining those two words together.

**Example**: [النمل:15] قَالَا الْحَمْدُ لِلَّهِ , in this example the letter of *madd* will be dropped in pronunciation when joining with the following word, الْحَمْدُ, as it has a *saakin* on the first letter, (ل).

(11) There are many more different situations of *madd* mentioned in certain books when the aforementioned fourteen situations are multiplied with the different methods of doing *waqf* (stopping & pausing). These situations are very briefly indicated in the notes within this book; however, the detailed version of these situations can be searched in various other books of *tajweed*.

## The categories of *Madd* in الحروف الهجائيّة:

الحروف الهجائيّة refer to the different individual letters of the alphabet. There are certain chapters in the *Qur'an* where the beginnings of those chapters are recited as individual letters of the alphabet.

**Example**: [مريم:1] كهيعص , this will be read as five individual letters.

In total there are 14 different letters that occur at the beginning of the different chapter's. The lengths of the different letters can differ. Some will be recited with 6 *harakaat* and others will be recited with a shorter length.

These 14 different letters can be divided into **four** categories according to their lengths as indicated in the table below:

|   | Length | Which letters? | Amount of letters? |
|---|--------|----------------|--------------------|
| 1 | 6 *harakaat* | (س)(ن)(ق)(ص)(ل)(م)(ك) | 7 |
| 2 | 6 or 4 *harakaat* | (ع) | 1 |
| 3 | 2 *harakaat* | (ح)(ي)(ط)(ه)(ر) | 5 |
| 4 | No madd | (ا) | 1 |

# The different levels of المدّ الفرعي:

Five different types of المدّ الفرعي have been mentioned above. These different types of المدّ الفرعي have different levels of strength. Some types are stronger than others. Therefore, when there are two (or more) types gathered together in one word, then the length of المدّ الفرعي will be based upon the stronger type. The strength of المدّ الفرعي is as follows: (starting with the strongest type)

|   | Type | Strength |
|---|------|----------|
| 1 | اللازم | Strongest |
| 2 | المتصل |  |
| 3 | العارض |  |
| 4 | المنفصل |  |
| 5 | البدل | Weakest |

Example: In the example [المائدة:2] وَلَا آمِّيْنَ الْبَيْتَ the word آمِّيْنَ has two types of المدّ الفرعي gathered. There is البدل in ( آ ) and there is اللازم as there is a *saakin* after the *hamzah*, hence in this word البدل and اللازم are both present. From the rules above the word should be stretched the duration of **two harakaat** due to البدل and the duration of **six harakaat** due to اللازم. Now, as both the *madd* have contradicting rulings, the ruling of اللازم will be given preference and applied as it is the **stronger** of the two types of *madd;* the ruling of البدل will be dropped.

**Note**: Many words will have a few types gathered like the example above, similar analysing will take place for other examples. **The rule of the stronger type of *madd* will always be acted upon.**

# *Waqf*

## Flowchart outlining the different discussions of *Waqf*:

The following flowchart outlines the chapters of '*Waqf*' – the different situations discussed within the chapter on the following pages:

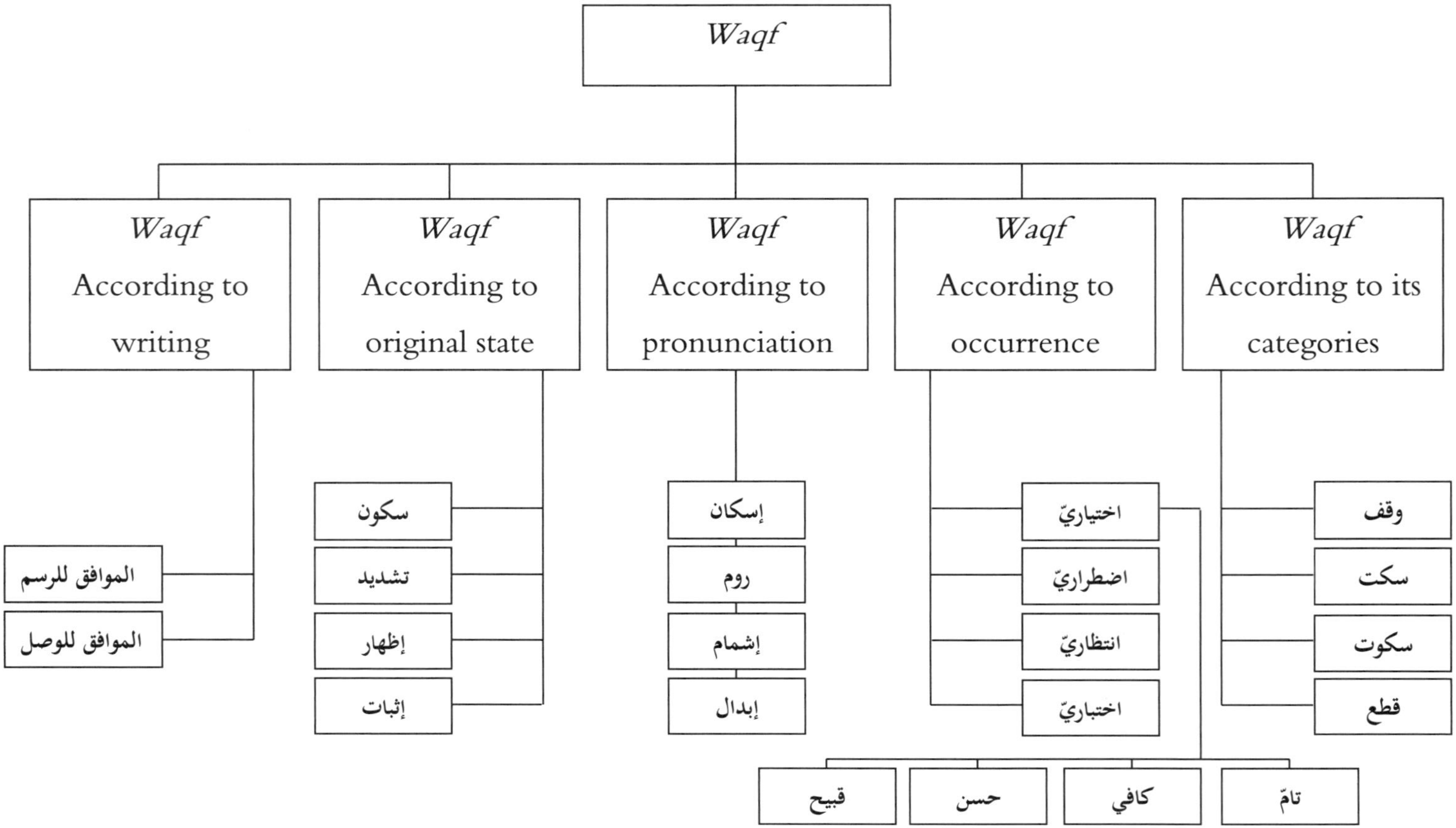

```
                                    Waqf
                                      │
    ┌─────────────┬──────────────┬────┴─────────┬──────────────┐
  Waqf          Waqf          Waqf            Waqf           Waqf
According to  According to  According to    According to   According to
  writing    original state pronunciation    occurrence     its categories
    │             │             │                │               │
 ┌──┴──┐      ┌──┬┴─┬──┐    ┌──┬┴─┬──┐      ┌──┬┴─┬──┐      ┌──┬┴─┬──┐
الموافق      سكون تشديد   إسكان  روم        اختياري اضطراري    وقف  سكت
 للرسم       إظهار إثبات   إشمام  إبدال      انتظاري اختياري    سكون قطع
الموافق
 للوصل
```

According to original state: سكون، تشديد، إظهار، إثبات

According to pronunciation: إسكان، روم، إشمام، إبدال

According to occurrence: اختياري، اضطراري، انتظاري، اختياري

According to its categories: وقف، سكت، سكون، قطع

Sub-categories: تام، كافي، حسن، قبيح

According to writing: الموافق للرسم، الموافق للوصل

# Waqf

The dictionary meaning of the term *waqf* is 'to stop'.

In the terminology of *tajweed*, the term *waqf* is divided into **four main categories**.

1) وَقْف (*waqf*)
2) سَكْت (*sakt*)
3) سُكُوْت (*sukoot*)
4) قَطْع (*qat'*)

The table below defines the categories of *waqf*:

|   | Term | Definition |
|---|------|------------|
| 1 | وَقْف | This is to stop the voice, recitation and the breath at the end of a word for a short period with the intention of starting the recitation again. |
| 2 | سَكْت | This is to stop the voice and recitation without breathing for a short period, thereafter continuing the recitation. |
| 3 | سُكُوْت | This is to stop the voice and recitation, breath at the end of the word for a long period (a period longer than needed for just breathing). Instead the pause is stretched for any reason; with the intention of continuing the recitation. |
| 4 | قَطْع | This is to stop the recitation completely with the intention of **not** continuing the recitation. |

**Notes**:

(1) *Waqf* can occur at the end of the verse even at the end of a word, however it cannot occur inbetween a word or two separate words which have been written as one in the Qur'an. Example: In the verse [سورة الحج:5] لِكَيْلَا يَعْلَمَ, it is **not permissible** to stop at the end of the word لِكَيْ despite it being an individual word itself. This is because the word كَيْ is joint in **writing** with the following word لَا, as لِكَيْلَا.

(2) It is **necessary** in *waqf* that the reciter takes a breath when pausing, if he does not take a breath when pausing then this will be regarded as *sakt*, **NOT** *waqf*.

(3) The length of pause during *waqf* should be as long as taking a breath with easiness; it is not good to lengthen the pause beyond this length as this could become similar to *sukoot*.

(4) A golden rule is **wasl is given preference over waqf;** hence, whenever *wasl* is possible and *waqf* is **not necessary**, *wasl* should be done.

(5) When doing *waqf* upon a letter which possesses one of the 'temporary qualities', then the 'quality' will **not** be expressed.

Example: In the verse [40:يوسف] سَيِّئُمُوْهَا أَنتُمْ , when stopping on the word سَيِّئُمُوْهَا then the *madd* will **not** be expressed. It is important that no extra sound or length is added to the *alif* when stopping upon it.

(6) It is **necessary** when doing *waqf* to make the last letter *saakin*, it is not permissible to pray the last letter as a *mutaharrik* **except** if the *waqf* completed is الوقف بالروم , (a discussion on this will come under the heading 'types of *waqf* according to pronunciation').

(7) It is **not permissible** to recite the *tanween* when doing *waqf*, instead it will be changed into a *saakin* or in certain situations الوقف بالإبدال will occur, (a discussion on this will come under the heading 'types of *waqf* according to pronunciation').

(8) In those places of the Qur'an where an indication of *waqf* and *sakt* is given, it is permissible to do *waqf* or *sakt;* however, it is **not permissible** to continue.

(9) It is **not permissible** to stop in a verse which contains the حروف مقطّعات (broken letters). If *waqf* is done on any of these letters due to need then it is necessary to repeat the verse from the beginning.

Example: In the verse [1:مريم] كهيعص if the reciter due to need stops on the letter (ع) then he will need to repeat the full verse again from the letter (ك).

(10) *Qat'* will **only occur at the end of the verses** within the Qur'an.

# Types of *Waqf* according to occurrence:

*waqf* can occur in four ways.

1) الوقف الاختياري (*waqf* done out of choice).
2) الوقف الاضطراري (*waqf* done due to need).
3) الوقف الانتظاري (*waqf* done to pray the different forms of *Qira'ah*).
4) الوقف الاختباري (*waqf* done to test).

The table below defines and gives an example for the categories of '*waqf* according to occurrence':

|   | Term | Definition | Example |
|---|------|------------|---------|
| 1 | اِخْتِيَارِيٌّ | This is when the reciter stops on a word without the occurrence of any cause, instead he stops on the word intentionally. This is (the reason) why it is given its name as the stop is **optional**. | Stopping on the word [العَذابَ:1] **optionally**. |
| 2 | اِضْطِرَارِيٌّ | This is when the reciter stops on a word due to force and need. For example he stops on a word due to lack of breath or due to forgetting the next word. This is (the reason) why it is given its name as the pause is **forceful**, not optional. | Stopping on the word [العَذابَ:5] due to a lack of breath; **forcefully**. |
| 3 | اِنْتِظَارِيٌّ | This is when the reciter stops on a word when praying the different narrations; he stops so that he can join the other narrations. This is (the reason) why it is given its name as the reciter is stopping and making one narration wait until he reads the other narration. | If the reciter stops on the word [العَذابَ:3] بِجٍ so that he can pray the two different methods of praying the word بِجٍ & بَلَىٰ before it. |
| 4 | اِخْتِبَارِيٌّ | This is when the teacher/questioner stops on a word so that he can test the students or the student stops on a word in order to answer the question posed to him by the teacher/questioner. | If the teacher asks the student to stop on the word [العَذابَ:3] بِجٍ to check how he does *waqf* upon the letter (ر). |

**Notes**:

(1) When stopping out of choice (الوقف الاختياري) it is **compulsory** to do *waqf* on a place which is suitable for pausing. (This will be discussed in the chapter 'types of الوقف الاختياري').

(2) When the **stopping** is due to force or need (الوقف الاضطراري), it is possible to stop **at the end of any word**, however it will be **compulsory** to restart from that word or any other word before.

# Types of 'الوقف الاختياري':

'الوقف الاختياري' is divided into **four** types.

(1) الوقف التّام
(2) الوقف الكافي
(3) الوقف الحسن
(4) الوقف القبيح

The table below defines the types of 'الوقف الاختياري':

|   | Term | Definition |
|---|------|------------|
| 1 | الوقف التّام | This is to pause on such a word which is not linked with the word after it, **not** in terms of syntax (grammar) and **not** in terms of meaning. Basically, the word paused upon is completely separate from the word after it. |
| 2 | الوقف الكافي | This is to pause on such a word which is **not linked** with the word after it in terms of syntax; however it is linked with the word after it in terms of meaning. |
| 3 | الوقف الحسن | This is to pause on such a word which is linked with the word after it in terms of syntax and meaning **with the condition that the stopping creates beauty within the recitation**. |
| 4 | الوقف القبيح | This is to pause on such a word which is linked with the word after it in terms of syntax and meaning **with the condition that the stopping does not create any beauty within the recitation** |

The table below gives examples and mentions the rulings of 'الوقف الاختياري':

| | Term | Example | Ruling |
|---|---|---|---|
| 1 | الوقف التام | Stopping on the word [5 : البقرة] المُفْلِحُونَ and then starting the recitation from the following verse which is [6 : البقرة] إِنَّ الَّذِينَ كَفَرُوا. Both the verses are completely **different** in terms of syntax and meaning. | It is **compulsory** to stop in these places and then start the recitation from the following word. |
| 2 | الوقف الكافي | Stopping on the word [6 : البقرة] لَا يُؤْمِنُونَ and then starting the recitation from the following verse which is خَتَمَ اللَّهُ عَلَى [7 : البقرة]. Both the verses are **different** in terms of syntax but are the **same** in terms of meaning. | It is **best** to stop in these places and then start the recitation from the following word. (*waqf* is based upon syntax link; hence *waqf* in this is **best**). |
| 3 | الوقف الحسن | Stopping on the phrase [1 : الفاتحة] الْحَمْدُ لِلَّهِ, stopping on the word اللَّهِ creates beauty within the recitation, however, the following words [1:الفاتحة] رَبِّ الْعَالَمِينَ is linked with the word اللَّهِ, both in terms of syntax and meaning. | When pausing on such words, it is best to repeat the word paused upon and then joining with the following word; **if the word paused upon is not the end of a verse**. However, if the word paused upon is at the end of a verse, despite the following verse linked to it in terms of syntax and meaning, it is **better** to start the recitation from the following word. For example, pausing on [1 : الفاتحة] الْحَمْدُ and then starting with [2 : الفاتحة] الرَّحْمَنُ. |
| 4 | الوقف القبيح | Stopping on the word بِسْمِ from بِسْمِ اللَّهِ creates no special meaning. Also, it is linked with the word after it in terms of syntax and meaning. Therefore, it would be bad to pause on such a word. | It is not permissible to stop on such words except for when there is a need; lack of breath, teaching students, etc. When pausing on such words it is **compulsory** to restart the recitation from the word paused upon (or any word prior to it), it is not permissible to continue the recitation from the following word. |

**Note**: If it is possible to stretch your breath until a place where الوقف التام or الكافي is possible then الوقف بالحسن or الوقف القبيح **should not be done**.

# Types of *Waqf* according to pronunciation:

*Waqf* is divided into **four** types 'according to pronunciation'.

1) الوقف بالسكّان
2) الوقف بالرّوم
3) الوقف بالإشمام
4) الوقف بالإبدال

The table below defines the categories of '*waqf* according to pronunciation':

| | Term | Definition |
|---|---|---|
| 1 | الوقف بالسكّان | This is to pray the letter upon which *waqf* has occurred on as *saakin*. **This occurs with any of the three *harakaat*.** |
| 2 | الوقف بالرّوم | This is to pray part of the *harakah* of the letter upon which *waqf* is done. Only part of the *harakah* will be prayed, such that only the person close realises the *harakah* but the person sitting far does not realise the *harakah* prayed. **This only happens with the *harakaat*; *dhammah* or *kasrah*.** |
| 3 | الوقف بالإشمام | This is to pray the letter upon which *waqf* has occurred on as *saakin*, however an indication to the *harakah* is made with the lips. **This only happens with the *harakah dhammah*.** |
| 4 | الوقف بالإبدال | This is to change the letter upon which *waqf* has occurred upon, into another letter. This occurs in two situations:<br>(1) To change a letter which ends in a *fathah with tanween* into a single *fathah* with an *alif* after it. Example: نَصِيرًا into نَصِيرَا.<br>(2) To change a letter which ends in a *round taa* into a *haa* when stopping. Example: جَنَّةٌ into جَنَّهْ. |

**Notes**:

(1) It is **not permissible** to do الوقف بالإشمام or الوقف بالروم in the following five cases:

| | Situation | Example |
|---|---|---|
| 1 | When the letter paused upon has السكون الأصليّ. | The word فَلَا تَنْهَرْ has a سكون أصليّ on the last letter, hence الروم or الإشمام is **not** allowed within it. |
| 2 | When the letter paused upon has الحركة العارضة. | The word مَنْ يُشَاقِقِ has a حركة عارضة on the last letter, hence الروم or الإشمام is **not** allowed within it. |
| 3 | When the letter paused upon is ميم الجمع. | The word عَلَيْهِمْ has a ميم الجمع on the last letter, hence الروم or الإشمام is **not** allowed within it. |
| 4 | When the letter paused upon is هاء التأنيث. | The word وَرَحْمَةُ has a هاء التأنيث on the last letter (when pausing), hence الروم or الإشمام is **not** allowed within it. |
| 5 | When the letter paused upon is هاء السكت. | The word لَمْ يَتَسَنَّهْ has a هاء السكت on the last letter, hence الروم or الإشمام is **not** allowed within it. |

(2) الوقف بالروم occurs with *dhammah* and *kasrah*. However, it is important to note that in الوقف بالروم *tanween* will not be prayed, instead the word which has a *tanween* will be read with a **single** *dhammah* or *kasrah*.

(3) In هاء الضمير the pause can be pronounced as الوقف بالروم, however in this case صلة will not occur. Example: In the verse [آل عمران: 101] وَفِيكُمْ رَسُولُهُ وَمَن يَعْتَصِم بِاللَّهِ, **when joining** the word رسولُهُ with the following word it will be read with صلة, hence pronounced as رَسُولُهُو وَمَن يَعْتَصِم. However, when doing *waqf* on this word it is not permissible to do صلة, instead it will simply be prayed as وَرَسُولُهُ with just pronouncing the *dhammah* slightly.

(4) It is important to note that within تاء التأنيث it is **permissible** to do الوقف بالروم. Example: In the [الممتحنة: 12] إِذَا جَاءَكَ الْمُؤْمِنَاتُ, it is **permissible** to do الوقف بالروم upon the تاء التأنيث (ت).

(5) It is permissible to do الوقف بالروم or الوقف بالإشمام upon a *mushaddad* letter. Example: The word [سورة البقرة: 36] عَدُوٌّ.

(6) If the letter paused upon is الميم الساكن or النون الساكن then *ghunnah* will occur. *Ghunnah* will occur even in the state of الوقف بالإشمام and الوقف بالروم. *Ghunnah* length will be the duration of *two harakaat*.

(7) If the word upon which *waqf* takes place has a سكون أصلي (permanent *sakin*) prior to it, then it is **better** to do الوقف بالروم, this will allow the *saakin* prior to it to be prayed clearly. However, if الوقف بالسكون takes place then it is important that both the letters are prayed with a clear *saakin* and is **not changed to a** *harakah*. Example: In the word [الدهر: 26] سَبِّحْهُ, when doing *waqf* upon the last letter with الوقف بالإسكان, both the last and second to last letter will have a *saakin* upon them; hence it is very important that both letters are prayed with a clear *saakin*.

(8) The rules regarding stopping on the letter (ر) in terms of praying it with a 'full mouth' or an 'empty mouth' will be based on the rules discussed in the chapter titled 'full mouth & empty mouth'. It is important to note that if الوقف بالروم takes place on the letter (ر) it will be treated as a *harakah* upon the (ر); hence the rules of *harakah* will be used.

(9) When stopping upon a letter which originally has a *fathah* upon it, it is permissible to pray it in the following **three** methods:

- الطول مع الإسكان
- التوسّط مع الإسكان
- القصر مع الإسكان

(10) When stopping upon a letter which originally has a *kasrah* upon it, it is permissible to pray it in the following **four** methods:

- الطول مع الإسكان
- التوسّط مع الإسكان
- القصر مع الإسكان
- القصر مع الروم

(11) When stopping upon a letter which originally has a *dhammah* upon it, it is permissible to pray it in the following **seven** methods:

- الطول مع الإسكان
- التوسّط مع الإسكان
- القصر مع الإسكان
- الطول مع الإشمام
- التوسّط مع الإشمام
- القصر مع الإشمام
- القصر مع الروم

# Types of *Waqf* according to its original state

*Waqf* when linked to its original state is divided into **four types** (meaning the state of the word or letter if there was no *waqf* occurring).

1) الوقف بالسكون
2) الوقف بالتشديد
3) الوقف بالإظهار
4) الوقف بالإثبات

The table below defines and mentions the rules of the categories of '*waqf* according to its original state':

| | Term | Definition & Rule |
|---|---|---|
| 1 | الوقف بالسكون | This is to do *waqf* on a letter which was **originally** (before *waqf*) a *saakin*. It is **not permissible** to express any *harakah* on this letter when doing *waqf* upon it; as it was **originally a *saakin***. |
| 2 | الوقف بالتشديد | This is to do *waqf* on a letter which was **originally *mushaddad***. This type of *waqf* **only** occurs with *mushaddad* letters. When pausing on these letters it will be read with the duration of two *harakaat* (as the *tashdeed* indicates upon a double letter). |
| 3 | الوقف بالإظهار | This is to do *waqf* on a letter which when joining with the following word is prayed with either *idghaam* or *ikhfaa*. When pausing on such a letter, it will be prayed **without** *idghaam* or *ikhfaa*; instead it will be read with *izhaar*. |
| 4 | الوقف بالإثبات | This is to do *waqf* on a 'letter of *madd*': it is **compulsory** to express the 'letter of *madd*' when pausing; this is irrelevant of why the 'letter of *madd*' was **not prayed** in the situation of *wasl*. When pausing on a 'letter of *madd*' (the letters ا, و, or ي). |

The table below gives an example for categories of '*waqf*' according to its original state':

| | Term | Example |
|---|---|---|
| 1 | الوقف بالسكون | In the verse [9: الضحى] فَلَا تَقْهَرْ , it was originally a *saakin*, therefore when doing *wasl* it will be read with a *saakin*. In both situations; *wasl* and *waqf* it will be prayed as [9: الضحى] فَلَا تَقْهَرْ , with a *saakin*. |
| 2 | الوقف بالتشديد | In the verse [2: القمر] مُسْتَمِرٌّ , when joining the letter (ر) with the following word, it will be read with a *tashdeed* and its normal *harakah*. However, when pausing upon the letter (ر) it will be read with a *saakin* with the duration of two *harakaat* to show that the letter is a *mushaddad* letter. |
| 3 | الوقف بالإظهار | In the verse [176: الأعراف] يَلْهَثْ ذَٰلِكَ , when joining (ث) will be read with *idghaam* (meaning the letter (ث) will be changed to the letter (ذ). However, when pausing upon the letter (ث) this letter will be prayed **without idghaam**, instead it will be read with the 'quality' of *izhaar*; as يَلْهَثْ. |
| 4 | الوقف بالإثبات | In the verse [71: البقرة] الْحَقَّ فَالْآنَ نَسْتَقِي , when doing *wasl* the verse will be prayed as نَسْتَقِي فَالْآنَ الْحَقَّ, dropping the letter (ي) . However, when doing *waqf* the letter (ي) will be expressed; it will be prayed as نَسْتَقِيْ. |

**Notes**:

(1) It is **not permissible** to name الوقف بالإسكان as إسكان as إسكان means 'to make *saakin*'; in الوقف بالسكون the last letter is already a *saakin*.

(2) When the letter which *waqf* is done upon is a letter of إدغام, إخفاء, the letter (م) or (ن) in these **four situations** الوقف بالإظهار **is necessary**.

(3) When the letter paused upon is from such a حروف المدّة which are not pronounced in the state of *wasl* due to 'two *saakin's* meeting' then the حروف المدّة will be pronounced during *waqf* upon this letter, الوقف بالإثبات will occur upon the letter.

Example: In the verse [36:38:البقرة], قُلْنَا اهْبِطُوا , during *wasl* it will be pronounced as قُلْنَ اهْبِطُوا **without the** *alif*. However, when pausing upon قُلْنَا the *alif* will be expressed, الوقف بالإثبات will occur.

(4) حروف المدّة which is **not written** in the text, such حروف المدّة will be expressed when doing *waqf* upon it; الوقف بالإثبات will occur.

Example: In the verse [61:الشعراء], فَلَمَّا تَرَاءَ الْجَمْعَانِ , the word تَرَاءَ is pronounced in *waqf* as تَرَاءَا.

(5) An *alif* which is **written** but not pronounced in the state of *wasl* will be expressed when pausing upon it, الوقف بالإثبات will occur.

Example: The verse [163:الأنعام] وَأَنَا أَوَّلُ الْمُسْلِمِينَ , will be read in the state of *wasl* as وَأَنَ أَوَّلُ الْمُسْلِمِينَ , however in the state of *waqf* it will be read as وَأَنَا.

(6) When doing *waqf* upon one of the letters of قلقلة (قطب جدّ) which also has a *tashdeed* upon it, then the *tashdeed* will be prayed first and then the 'quality' of قلقلة will be expressed.

Example: When doing *waqf* upon the word [53:يونس] أَحَقُّ , firstly due to the *tashdeed* the pause will be the length of **two** *harakaat*, then the 'quality' of قلقلة will be expressed.

# Types of *Waqf* according to رسم and وصل

Whenever *waqf* is generally done it will follow the رسم (writing) of the Qur'an, however, sometimes the rules of *waqf* differ from the writing, and instead the *waqf* will follow the method of recitation in *wasl* (continuing the recitation/not pausing).

There are two types of *waqf* when divided into the categories of رسم and وصل:

(1) اَلْوَقْفُ الْمُوَافِقُ لِلرَّسْمِ
(2) اَلْوَقْفُ الْمُوَافِقُ لِلْوَصْلِ

The table below defines and gives an example for the two types:

|   | Type | Definition | Example |
|---|------|------------|---------|
| 1 | الوقف الموافق للرسم | This is when the pronunciation during *waqf* follows the writing of the Qur'an. | وَتَظُنُّونَ بِاللَّهِ الظُّنُونَا (10) هُنَالِكَ [الأحزاب: 10-11] When stopping on the word الظنونا the *alif* at the end will be pronounced as it is present in writing, despite the *alif* not being pronounced when the word الظنون is **joint** with the following word هنالك. |
| 2 | الوقف الموافق للوصل | This is when the pronunciation during *waqf* follows the pronunciation which would have occurred in the situation of '**joining**'. | مِّن رِّبًا لِّيَرْبُوَا۟ فِي أَمْوَالِ النَّاسِ [الروم:39] When stopping on the word ليربوا the last *alif* will not be pronounced despite it being present in **writing**. Instead, the pronunciation of the *alif* will be dropped just like its pronunciation is dropped in the situation of '**joining**'. |

**Notes**:

(1) Many times the pronunciation during *waqf* is similar to that of **writing** and '**joining**'. This is also called الوقف الموافق للرسم. An example for this is the word [الحاقة:25] كِتَابِيَهْ, this is pronounced when '**joining**' and **pausing** as it is written.

(2) In those places where according to قراءة (recitation passed on through generations) the *alif* written is just not pronounced, then this *alif* will be ignored at the time of *waqf* as well. Example: كَانَتْ قَوَارِيرَا۠ (15) قَوَارِيرَا۠ مِن فِضَّةٍ [الدهر:15-16], in this example the **second** قواريرا is written **with an *alif***, however according to the recitation of Imam *Hafs* it is **never** prayed with an *alif*, hence even during *waqf* the *alif* will not be pronounced despite it being written in the Qur'an.

(3) Those letters of *madd* which are prayed when '**joining**' but are not present in **writing will be prayed and expressed when *waqf* is done upon them**.

Example: [الزخرف:13] لِتَسْتَوُۥا عَلَىٰ ظُهُورِهِ , in this example the word لتستوا is written with a single *waaw*, however when pronounced it is pronounced as لِتَسْتَوُوا, hence when doing *waqf* upon this word the double *waaw* will be pronounced.

(4) In the word [4:الدهر] سَلَٰسِلَا۠ , when doing *waqf* it is permissible to follow the **writing** hence pause with an *alif* at the end, سَلَٰسِلَا۠. Also, it is permissible to pause on this word according to the pronunciation of '**joining**', hence dropping the *alif*, سَلَٰسِلْ.

# Signs of *Waqf* and signs of *Wasl*

In most scripts of the Qur'an there are certain signs and indications made for *waqf* and *wasl*. The table below mentions most of these signs:

| | Sign | Meaning & Rule |
|---|---|---|
| 1 | ○ | This sign is referred to as an آيَة (verse). It is Sunnah to pause on these places. In terms of the *waqf* rules, it is **preferable** to pause on these places, **not compulsory**. This is because this sign sometimes occur where there is still a grammatical link with the following verse. However, if the reciter wants to express the different verses in his recitation then it will become compulsory to pause on this sign. |
| 2 | ۵ | This sign is referred to as an آية مختلف فيه (disputed verse). There are certain places in the Qur'an where the scholars have disputed whether it is the end of the verse or not, on such places where the scholars have disputed this sign will appear. It is **permissible** to continue reading when this sign appears or to treat it like complete verses and hence stop. |
| 3 | م | This sign is referred to as وقف لازم (compulsory pause). It is **compulsory** to pause when this sign appears; doing *wasl* when this sign appears could cause a weakness in meaning. |
| 4 | ط | This sign is referred to as وقف مطلق (unconditional pause). It is **compulsory** to pause when this sign appears; doing *wasl* when this sign appears could cause a weakness in meaning. |
| 5 | ج | This sign is referred to as وقف جائز (permissible pause). It is **good to pause** when this sign appears to decorate the recitation and to create an effect within the meaning. |
| 6 | ز | This sign is referred to as وقف مُجَوَّز (accepted pause). It is **permissible** to pause upon this sign when the signs mentioned above (first five signs) are far away and the reciter wants breath. This is regarded as a **weak sign** for the indication of pausing. |
| 7 | ص | This sign is referred to as وقف مُرَخَّص (authorised pause). It is **permissible** to pause upon this sign only at the time of need. This is also regarded as a **weak sign** for the indication of pausing. |
| 8 | ق | This sign is referred to as قِيْلَ عَلَيْهِ الْوَقْف (pause has been mentioned for it). It is **permissible** to pause upon this sign, however this sign is also regarded as a **weak sign** for the indication of pausing. |
| 9 | ك | This sign is referred to as كَذَلِك (the same as before). **This sign indicates that the ruling of pausing in this place is exactly the same as the last sign**. If the last sign was a sign which indicated upon pausing then a pause |

| | | |
|---|---|---|
| | | should be done in this place as well. If the last sign was an indication that pausing is not allowed then it is not permissible to pause in this place as well. |
| 10 | قَفْ | This sign is referred to as قَدْ يُوْقَفَ (pause has been done upon it). This sign indicates that it is **permissible** to pause upon this place. However, it is **not good** to do an optional pause on this sign. |
| 11 | صَلْ | This sign is referred to as قَدْ يُوْصَل (wasl has been done upon it). This sign indicates that it is **permissible** to pause upon this sign. However, it is **better not to pause**, instead it is preferred to do wasl upon these signs. |
| 12 | صلى | This sign is referred to as الوصل أولى (wasl is better). This sign indicates that it is best to do wasl in these places, if waqf is done in these places then it is compulsory to repeat the previous word and thereafter continue the recitation. |
| 13 | لَا | This sign is referred to as لا وقف عليه (no waqf here). This sign indicates that it is **not permissible** to pause on this place. Stopping on this place could change the context and meaning completely into a wrong explanation of the verse. |
| 14 | قِلَا | This sign is referred to as "قيل لا وقف عليه" or "وقف مختلف فيه". This sign indicates that doing waqf in these places is disputed amongst scholars, however **majority say it is better not to do waqf in these places**. The scholars who say waqf can be done mention that إعادة (repeating the verse) does not need to be done, instead continue from the following word. |
| 15 | لا ○ | This sign is referred to as "آية لا وقف عليه". This sign indicates that due to it being the end of a verse, an *ayah;* it is allowed (instead it is a practice of the Prophet) to do waqf upon this place. However, according to the rules of *tajweed* & *waqf* it is better not to stop as the two sentences are still grammatically linked. Therefore, the reciter has an option in this place to pause, however if he pauses he will not to إعادة instead he will do ابتداء (start from the following verse). |
| 16 | ∴ ∴ | This sign is referred to as "وقف معانقة". This sign will occur in pairs. Also, when this sign is written, on the side of the Qur'an there will be "مع" written. This sign indicates that in the two places that this sign occurs, you will not do waqf on both places because the sentence inbetween will lose its link to the sentences. Also, you will not do wasl on both places as this could confuse the listener in understanding the meaning. An example is given below: <br> لَا رَيْبَ ∴ فِيْهِ ∴ هُدًى لِلْمُتَّقِيْنَ [البقرة:2] |

| | | |
|---|---|---|
| 17 | وَقْفَه | This sign is referred to as "الوقف مع السكت". This sign indicates that if *sakt* is done in this place then the pause should be of similar duration to that of *waqf*, not shorter. It is also permissible to do *waqf* in this place. However, it is not permissible to do a **short** *sakt* in this place. |
| 18 | وَقْفُ النَّبِيّ | This sign is referred to as 'those places where Prophet ﷺ did *waqf* inbetween a verse'. There were certain places where continuously the Prophet paused, scholars mention there are eleven places in the Qur'an where this occurs. In this place it is **preferable** to pause. |
| 19 | وَقْفُ مُنَزَّل | This is also called وقف جبرائيل. These indicates to those places where the angel جبرائيل paused (other than the end of verses) when coming down with the revelation. In this place it is **preferable** to pause. |
| 20 | وَقْفُ غُفْرَان | This sign is referred to as 'places where stopping creates happiness and hope of forgiveness'. In this place *waqf* is **preferred** over *wasl*. |
| 21 | وَقْفُ كُفْرَان | This sign is referred to as 'places where pausing could create a wrong meaning and a belief within the listener that may lead to *kufr*'. It is **strongly recommended not to pause** upon such signs as the listener may understand the wrong meaning. |

**Notes**:

(1) There are certain places as indicated where scholars have unanimously said that *waqf* can be done in those places. These places will always be given preference over the places where scholars have disputed regarding the ruling of *waqf*.

(2) There are certain signs of *waqf* which are regarded stronger and certain which are regarded weaker. Doing *waqf* upon stronger signs is given preference over weaker signs. (The strongest sign for *waqf* is (م) and the weakest sign is (صلى). The order of the list is mostly in order of the strongest to the weakest sign).

(3) After doing *waqf* on a word it is important to know whether the word paused upon will be recited again or will the recitation continue from the following word. The signs above indicate what should be done.

(4) There are three signs which strongly indicate that *waqf* should **not be done** in these places. These signs are (لا) then (وقف كُفْرَان) and then (صلى).

(5) When the reciter is praying the Qur'an slowly (تَرْتِيل), the reciter should do *waqf* on all the places where *waqf* is permissible.

(6) When the reciter is praying the Qur'an quickly (حَدْر), the reciter should **not** do *waqf* on all the signs of *waqf*; instead he should only do *waqf* in the necessary places and at the time of need.

(7) When the reciter is praying the Qur'an with an inbetween speed (تَدْوِير), the reciter should do *waqf* in the places where a strong sign appears and he should do *wasl* in the places where a weak sign appears.

(8) There are differences amongst scholars regarding the placement of signs in certain places; however, it is important to note that stopping in the wrong place despite being **not permissible**, **will not result in a sin** if the stopping is not done with a bad intention. The reciter simply has to repeat the recitation from a suitable place.

# Types & Rules of *Sakt*

The definition of سَكْت (*sakt*) is to stop the voice and recitation without breathing for a short period, thereafter continuing the recitation.

Generally the sign (سَكْت), (سَكْتَة) or (س) is written in the places where *sakt* is permissible.

According to the narration of Imam *Hafs*, *sakt* is **compulsory** in four places within the Qur'an. The following table mentions the **four compulsory places** for *sakt*:

| | Four places **compulsory** for *sakt* |
|---|---|
| 1 | وَلَمْ يَجْعَلْ لَهُ عِوَجًا (سكت) قَيِّمًا [سورة الكهف : 1-2] |
| 2 | مَنْ بَعَثَنَا مِنْ مَرْقَدِنَا (سكت) هَذَا مَا وَعَدَ الرَّحْمَنُ [سورة يس : 52] |
| 3 | وَقِيلَ مَنْ (سكت) رَاقٍ [سورة القيامة : 27] |
| 4 | بَلْ (سكت) رَانَ [سورة المطففين : 14] |

**Note**: According to Imam *Jazri*, etc, there is also تَرْكُ السَّكْت in these four places.

According to the scholars there are **only four places** where *sakt* is allowed inbetween the verse. The following table mentions the **four places** where *sakt* is **permissible** according to the scholars:

| | Four places **permissible** for *sakt* |
|---|---|
| 1 | رَبَّنَا ظَلَمْنَا أَنْفُسَنَا (سكت) وَإِن لَّمْ تَغْفِرْ [الأعراف : 23] |
| 2 | أَوَلَمْ يَتَفَكَّرُوا (سكت) مَا بِصَاحِبِهِم [الأعراف : 184] |
| 3 | أَعْرِضْ عَنْ هَذَا (سكت) وَاسْتَغْفِرِي لِذَنبِكِ [يوسف : 29] |
| 4 | حَتَّى يُصْدِرَ الرِّعَاءُ (سكت) وَأَبُونَا شَيْخٌ كَبِيرٌ [القصص : 23] |

**Notes**:

(1) *Sakt* is a type of *waqf*, hence **majority** of the rules of *sakt* and *waqf* will be similar.

(2) The pause duration in *sakt* will be **less** than the duration of pause within *waqf*.

(3) In *sakt* it is **permissible** to do روم or إشمام; however, **it is best not to do it**.

(4) It is important to **refrain** from doing *sakt* anywhere other than the places where *sakt* is permissible.

(5) After doing *sakt*, the reciter will do ابتداء, it is **not permissible** to do إعادة.

(6) In those places where there is هاء السكت at the end of the word, it is **not permissible** to do *sakt* when it occurs inbetween verses. If they occur at the end of verses then it is permissible.

The هاء السكت occurs **seven times** within the Qur'an.

| | Seven places where هاء السكت is written |
|---|---|
| 1 | لَمْ يَتَسَنَّهْ [البقرة : 259] |
| 2 | اقْتَدِهْ [الأنعام : 90] |
| 3 | كِتَابِيَهْ [الحاقّة : 19] |
| 4 | حِسَابِيَهْ [الحاقّة : 20] |
| 5 | مَالِيَهْ [الحاقّة : 28] |
| 6 | سُلْطَانِيَهْ [الحاقّة : 29] |
| 7 | مَاهِيَهْ [القارعة : 10] |

(7) In the verse مَالِيَهْ [الحاقّة : 28] there is contradiction between scholars whether it is compulsory to do *sakt* or not.

# Types & Rules of *Sukoot*

The definition of سُكُوْت (sukoot) is to stop the voice and recitation, breath at the end of the word for a long period. A period longer than the amount needed for standard breathing; due to some reason, **with the intention** of continuing the recitation.

**There are certain rules to consider when doing *sukoot*:**

(1) It is important that the reciter, who temporarily stops recitation, has an intention of continuing the recitation; **the reciter has not stopped reciting completely**.

(2) The pause in *sukoot* will be longer than normal *waqf*.

(3) The rules of *sukoot* are the same as *waqf*. Even if the *sukoot* is very long, the reciter does **not** need to pray اِستعاذة again.

(4) If the reciter talks about something other than the Qur'an whilst doing *sukoot* then the *sukoot* will break; hence recitation is finished. Therefore, if he restarts the recitation it will be assumed that he is starting the recitation from the beginning, hence it will be **compulsory** to adhere to the rules of 'starting recitation'; praying اِستعاذة, etc.

(5) Even if a long time has passed, the reciter has moved places, etc, the ruling of *sukoot* will remain with the condition that his mind is focussed on recitation as the reciter will be assumed to be in the state of recitation.

(6) When teaching, also explaining *tajweed* rules, explanation of verses, etc, the state of *sukoot* will remain, hence there is no need to pray اِستعاذة when starting the recitation again.

(7) *Sukoot* should only occur at the end of verses, **not inbetween verses**.

(8) It is **not permissible** to do *sukoot* in those places where *sakt* is compulsory.

# Types & Rules of *Qat'*

The definition of قَطْع (*qat'*) is to stop the recitation completely **with the intention of not continuing the recitation**.

### There are certain rules to consider when doing *qat'*:

(1) If the reciter pauses in the recitation for a long period with the intention of continuing (he did *sukoot*); however, he never continued praying, this will eventually become *qat'*.

(2) If the reciter has an intention to stop the recitation, this is called القطع الحقيقيّ (real break).

(3) If the reciter never had an intention to stop the recitation; however, during the recitation a situation occurred where he had to stop his recitation, or he did some act which would be regarded against continuous recitation then this break is called القطع الاتّفاقيّ.

(4) After the occurrence of any form of *qat'* it is compulsory to pray استعاذة again when starting the recitation.

(5) It is not compulsory that when the reciter completes the Qur'an he stops the recitation and performs *qat'*, therefore it is not necessary to pray استعاذة again after completing the Qur'an if the reciter had an intention to continue.

(6) *Qat'* is a type of *waqf* hence most of the rules of *waqf* will apply to *qat'*.

(7) It is permissible to do *qat'* at the end of any verse, however it is better to do *qat'* upon those places where the letter (ع) is written on the margin of the Qur'an or to do *qat'* at the end of the chapter.

(8) Upon those verses where there is a sign of *wasl*, **it is better not to do *qat'***.

(9) It is **not permissible** to do *qat'* on those signs of *waqf* which occur inbetween the verses.

# The three stages of recitation

There are **three famous** stages of recitation:

1. تَرْتِيْل
2. حَدَر
3. تَدْوِيْر

The following table defines each type:

|   | Stage | Definition |
|---|-------|------------|
| 1 | تَرْتِيْل | This is to recite slowly, such that each letter is clearly recited from its 'place of pronunciation' and all the 'qualities' of each letter are made clear. Further, the speed is such that the meaning can be comprehended whilst reciting. |
| 2 | حَدَر | This is to recite quickly whilst following the rules of *tajweed* and recitation properly. |
| 3 | تَدْوِيْر | This is the speed of recitation which is inbetween ترتيل and حدر. |

**Notes**:

(1) تدوير is sometimes referred to as تَجْوِيْد.

(2) Some scholars have indicated to another type, namely تَحْقِيْق. In reality this type is very similar to ترتيل ; the difference is that ترتيل is to pray slowly for increasing contemplation and تحقيق is praying slowly for learning and improving recitation.

(3) There is a type which is forbidden, namely هَذْرَمَة. This is to recite quicker than حَدَر without fully adopting the rules of recitation.

# Hamzah

## Types of *Hamzah*

The letter *hamzah* has some further rules compared to the other letters; depending upon the state of the *hamzah*.

There are two types of *hamzah*:

(1) هَمْزَةُ الْوَصْل (joining *hamzah*) – this is also known as هَمْزَةُ الْعَارِض (temporary *hamzah*)

(2) هَمْزَةُ الْأَصْل (original *hamzah*) – this is also known as هَمْزَةُ الْقَطْع (permanent *hamzah*)

The following table defines each type of *hamzah*:

|   | Type | Definition |
|---|---|---|
| 1 | هَمْزَةُ الْوَصْل (هَمْزَةُ الْعَارِض) | This is such a *hamzah* which is **only** recited when the recitation begins from it; it is **dropped** when the recitation is continuing from a letter before. |
| 2 | هَمْزَةُ الْأَصْل (هَمْزَةُ الْقَطْع) | This is such a *hamzah* which is recited in both situations; when starting the recitation from it and when continuing the recitation from a letter before. |

Below an example for each type of *hamzah* is given with a brief explanation.

Example for a 'joining/temporary *hamzah*': اضْرِبْ بِعَصَاكَ الْحَجَرَ [البقرة:60], in this example the *hamzah* at the beginning of the word اضْرِبْ is a 'joining/temporary *hamzah*'.

Example for an 'original/permanent *hamzah*': أَحْسَنَ الْقَصَصِ [يوسف:3], in this example the *hamzah* at the beginning of the word أَحْسَنَ is an 'original/permanent *hamzah*'.

# Rules of *Hamzah*

The two types of *hamzah*'s mentioned above have certain rules which are mentioned in the table below with examples:

| | Rule | Example |
|---|---|---|
| 1 | Whenever there is a **mutaharrik** 'permanent *hamzah*'; it will **always** be prayed **clearly**. | [1 :المؤمنون] قَدْ أَفْلَحَ It is important that the *hamzah* at the beginning of the word أَفْلَحَ is read **clearly**; making sure the *hamzah* **does not** change into an *alif*. |
| 2 | Extra care should be taken when two *mutaharrik hamzah's* occur next to each other; both should be prayed **clearly** and **distinctly**. | [6 :التحريم] التَّلجِئَةُ In this word both the *hamzah*'s that appear at the beginning should be prayed **very clearly**; making sure the *hamzah* **does not** change into an *alif*. |
| 3 | Whenever the recitation starts from a 'joining/temporary *hamzah*', this *hamzah* will be recited; however, if the recitation is continued from the words before, this *hamzah* will be dropped in recitation. | The phrase [4 :عمران آل] ذُو انتِقَامٍ has a 'joining *hamzah*' at the beginning of the word انتِقَامٍ. This will be read as ذُو انتِقَامٍ when continuing from the word before, and it will be read as إنتِقَامٍ if recitation starts from the word itself. |
| 4 | Whenever a **saakin** 'permanent *hamzah*' occurs after a *mutaharrik hamzah*; it is necessary to change the *saakin hamzah* according to the letter of the *harakah* before. | [13 :البقرة] ءَامَنُوا – notice the *hamzah* has changed to an *alif*.<br>[283 :البقرة] أُوتُمِنَ – notice the *hamzah* has changed to a *waaw*.<br>[2 :الانسان] نَبتَلِيهِ – notice the *hamzah* has changed to a *yaa*. |
| 5 | Whenever the 'joining *hamzah*' is read; the *harakah* upon it changes according to the situation:<br>• It will be read with a *fathah* upon it when occurring before the letter *laam*.<br>• It will be read with a *dhammah* upon it when occurring before such a verb which has a *dhammah* upon its third letter.<br>• It will be read with a *kasrah* in all other situations. | [3 :البقرة] الَّذِينَ – notice the *hamzah* is a *fathah*.<br>[26 :ابراهيم] اجتُثَّتْ – notice the *hamzah* is a *dhammah*.<br>[118 :الأنعام] اسْمُ – notice the *hamzah* is a *kasrah*. |

**Notes**:

(1) The phrase 'according to the letter of the *harakah* before' means if the *harakah* before the *saakin* letter is a *fathah*, it will be changed to an *alif*, if it is a *dhammah*, it will be changed to a *waaw* and if it is a *kasrah*, it will be changed to a *yaa*.

(2) Rule number 2 mentioned that when two *mutaharrik hamzah's* occur next to each other, both should be prayed clearly. However, according to the narration of Imam *Hafs* there is one place within the Qur'an, the word [44:سجدة حم] ءَاَعۡجَمِيٌّ , where both of the *hamzah's* will not be prayed clearly; instead in the **second hamzah, tasheel will occur**.

*Tasheel* is praying the *hamzah* in such a manner that the noise created is inbetween *hamzah* and an *alif*; it is important to practice this with a person equipped in Qura'nic recitation.

(3) According to the aforementioned rule number 4; when a *saakin hamzah* appears after a *mutaharrik hamzah*, it is necessary to change the *saakin hamzah* according to the *harakah* of the letter before. However, it must be noted here that if the first *mutaharrik hamzah* is a 'joining/temporary *hamzah*' then it will only be read if the reciter starts the recitation with it; if the reciter is continuing the recitation from the previous word(s) then this type of *hamzah* will be omitted and hence the *saakin hamzah* will remain unchanged.

Example: [الأحقاف: 4] فِي السَّمَاوَاتِ ائۡتُونِي , in this example there is a *saakin hamzah* in the word ائۡتُونِي after a 'joining/temporary *hamzah*'. Now, if the reciter starts reading this sentence from the word ائۡتُونِي itself; the reciter will change the *saakin hamzah* into a *yaa* as it will appear after another *mutaharrik hamzah* which is the 'joining/temporary *hamzah*' – it will be prayed as إِيتُونِي. However, if the reciter does not start the recitation from the word ائۡتُونِي, instead the reciter continues the recitation from the words before, the reciter reads as فِي السَّمَاوَاتِ ائۡتُونِي then the 'joining/temporary *hamzah*' will be dropped and the *saakin hamzah* will remain unchanged – it will be read as فِي السَّمَاوَاتِ ئۡتُونِي .

(4) In the rules above it is indicated that whenever there is a 'joining *hamzah*' at the beginning of a word; however, if the reciter is continuing the recitation from the previous word; then the 'joining *hamzah*' is omitted in reading. There is one exception to this case: If the 'joining *hamzah*' which has a *fathah* upon it follows a '*hamzah istifhaam*' (a *hamzah* which is used for questioning in the Arabic language) then the 'joining *hamzah*' will not be omitted; instead there are two possible methods of reciting this situation:

- Do *ibdaal* in the second *hamzah* – **this is the preferred option**.
- Do *tasheel* in the second *hamzah*

Example: The word [النمل:59] آللَّهُ has two *hamzah's* at the beginning of the word; the first is '*hamzah istifhaam*' and the second is a 'joining *hamzah*'; according to the normal rules the 'joining *hamzah*' is omitted. However, here as the 'joining *hamzah*' has a *fathah* upon it, the *hamzah* will not be omitted. Instead it will be read with *ibdaal;* as آﷲ , the *hamzah* is **changed** into an *alif*. Alternatively, the second *hamzah* can be read with *tasheel*, this is praying the *hamzah* in such a manner that the noise created is inbetween *hamzah* and an *alif;* it is important to practice this with a person equipped in Qura'nic recitation.

(5) If a 'joining *hamzah*' which **does not have fathah upon it** occurs after a '*hamzah istifhaam*', then according to the normal rules of 'joining *hamzah*' it will be dropped in reading. However, in addition to being dropped in reading, the 'joining *hamzah*' will also be dropped in writing in this specific situation.

Example: In the word [8:السبأ] أَإِفْتَرَى , the second *hamzah* is a 'joining *hamzah*' which is **not a fathah**, this occurs after a '*hamzah istifhaam*'; hence the 'joining *hamzah*' will be omitted in both; reading and writing. The word will be written and pronounced as أَفْتَرَى.

(6) In rule number 5 it mentioned that the 'joining/temporary *hamzah*' will be read with a *dhammah* upon it if the third letter of the verb is also a *dhammah;* however, there are some exceptions to this rule. In the word اِمْشُوا , despite the third letter of the verb having a *dhammah* upon it, the *hamzah* will be read with a *kasrah* upon it; not a *dhammah*. This is because the *dhammah* upon the third letter is temporary, it was originally a *kasrah*. This can be researched more in grammar books. It must be noted that these situations are very limited within the Qur'an; it is best to practice this by a person who is equipped with Qura'nic recitation.

# Method of reciting *Saakin*

It is important that the *saakin* is recited according to the proper method; this will ensure the recitation is performed in the best method.

The following table mentions the method of reciting *saakin*:

|   | Type | Method of recitation |
|---|------|----------------------|
| 1 | ْ  *Saakin* | *Saakin* should be recited by closing the mouth (to a different level for each letter) and closing the noise. However, the closing of the noise should be very short; immediately moving onto the next letter. |

**Note**: A *saakin* is also called *sukoon*.

# Method of reciting the different *Harakaat*

It is important that the different *harakaat* are recited according to the proper method; this will ensure the recitation is performed in the best method.

The following table mentions the method of reciting each *harakah*:

|   | *Harakah* | Method of recitation |
|---|---|---|
| 1 | ´<br>—<br>*Fathah* | *Fathah* should be recited with an open mouth. |
| 2 | ,<br>—<br>*Dhammah* | *Dhammah* should be recited with the closing of the lips. |
| 3 | —<br>*Kasrah* | *Kasrah* should be recited with the lowering of the mouth. |

**Notes**:

(1) A letter which has a *harakah* upon it is called a *mutaharrik*.

(2) The plural for the word *harakah* is *harakaat*.

(3) It is important to pray each *harakah* in its correct method; also extra care should be taken in **not** making a *saakin* into a *mutaharrik* and vice versa.

(4) After a *fathah* if there is no *alif*, after a *dhammah* if there is no *waaw* and after a *kasrah* if there is no *yaa*, then extra care should be taken that these letters are **not added**. Adding these letters is against the rules of recitation. Example: The word [البقرة:36] عَدُوٌ **should not** be pronounced as عَادُوٌ.

(5) It is very important to practice the recitation of these *harakaat* with a tutor who is equipped with Qura'nic recitation.

# Method of reciting *Tashdeed*

It is important that *tashdeed* is recited according to the proper method; this will ensure the recitation is performed in the best method.

The following table mentions the method of reciting *tashdeed*:

| | Type | Method of recitation |
|---|---|---|
| 1 | ّ *Tashdeed* | *Tashdeed* should be recited according to the 'place of pronunciation' of the second letter. The duration of the recitation of a letter with *tashdeed* should be slightly less than the duration of reciting two letters **without** *tashdeed*. |

**Notes**:

(1) A letter which has a *tashdeed* upon it is called *mushaddad*.

(2) Some scholars have mentioned the duration of *tashdeed* as two letters; however, the more accurate length is slightly less than two *mutaharrik* letters.

(3) It is important to merge the two letters together in recitation in the presence of a *tashdeed*.

(4) When two letters are merged and written with a *tashdeed* upon it; the first of the two letters will be regarded as a *saakin* letter and the second will be regarded as a *mutaharrik* letter.

(5) After two letters are merged together and written with a *tashdeed*; the second letter is regarded as the 'leading letter' and the first letter is regarded as a 'following letter'. Therefore, in most of the recitation 'qualities' of a *mushaddad* letter, the rules will be based upon the second letter.

# Imala'a

*Imala'a* ( إِمَالَة ) is a unique rule of recitation. This occurs when an *alif* follows a *fathah*, however the word is not recited in the normal method. Instead the *fathah* will be pronounced inbetween a *fathah* and *kasrah*, the *alif* will be pronounced inbetween an *alif* and a *yaa*.

This occurs many times in the seven (or more) different methods of recitation, however, according to the narration of Imam *Hafs* it only occurs once within the Qur'an.

The word مَجْرَاهَا in the verse [41:هود] بِسْمِ اللَّهِ مَجْرَاهَا وَمُرْسَاهَا , will be read with *imala'a* according to the recitation of Imam *Hafs*. It is important to practice this with a tutor who is equipped with Qura'nic recitation.

# Rules for *Tanween*

*Tanween* was discussed briefly in the chapter of '*noon saakin* and *tanween*'. Here further rules regarding *tanween* will be mentioned after its definition.

## Definition of *Tanween*

*Tanween* is an **extra *noon saakin*** at the end of a word, which is present in speaking but **not present** in writing or when pausing upon the *noon*.

Therefore, *tanween* is sometimes referred to as نون التنوين (The *noon* for *tanween*).

## Rules for *Tanween*

- *Tanween* is omitted in recitation when doing *waqf* upon it.
- Recitation can **never** begin with a *tanween*.
- If the *tanween* is a double *fathah* ( ً ) then it will be written with an *alif* after it.
  Example: The word [النساء:133] قَدِيرًا , will have an *alif* written after it as it has a double *fathah*.
- When the letter after the *tanween* is a 'joining *hamzah*', in continuous recitation the 'joining *hamzah*' will be omitted in recitation; instead the '*noon* for *tanween*' will be recited with a *kasrah* upon it.
  Example: The word [الصافات:6] بِزِينَةٍ ends with a *tanween*, the following word is الْكَوَاكِبِ , which starts with a 'joining *hamzah*'; when joining these two words together they will be recited as بِزِينَةٍ نِ الْكَوَاكِبِ. In some scripts of the Qur'an the small *noon* is written to make it easy for the readers.

# Meeting of two *Saakin's*

When two *saakin's* appear next to each other in text; sometimes, **both** the *saakin's* will be recited and sometimes one of the *saakin's* will be omitted in recitation.

There are two types of 'meeting of two *saakin's*':

(1) اِجْتِمَاعُ السَّاكِنَيْنِ عَلَى حَدِّهِ

(2) اِجْتِمَاعُ السَّاكِنَيْنِ عَلَى غَيْرِ حَدِّهِ

The table below explains each type and mentions an example:

|   | Type | Explanation | Example |
|---|------|-------------|---------|
| 1 | اِجْتِمَاعُ السَّاكِنَيْنِ عَلَى حَدِّهِ | This is when two *saakin's* come together **in one word** and the first **is** one of the 'letters of *madd*'. | دَآبَّة |
| 2 | اِجْتِمَاعُ السَّاكِنَيْنِ عَلَى غَيْرِ حَدِّهِ | This is when two *saakin's* appear next to each other in separate words **or** the first **is not** one of the 'letters of *madd*'. | أَقِيمُوا ٱلصَّلَاة |

**Note**: The rules for the meeting of two saakin's are mentioned below.

# Rules for 'meeting of two *Saakin's*'

There are certain rules for when two *saakin's* appear next to each other; depending on the type it is from. The rules are mentioned below:

(1) It is **permissible** according to **all scholars** to recite two *saakin's* together if it is from the category of اِجْتِمَاعُ السَّاكِنَيْنِ عَلَى حَدِّهِ .

(2) It is **not permissible** to recite two *saakin's* together if it is from the category of اِجْتِمَاعُ السَّاكِنَيْنِ عَلَى غَيْرِ حَدِّهِ , unless *waqf* is done upon the word.

(3) If in اِجْتِمَاعُ السَّاكِنَيْنِ عَلَى غَيْرِ حَدِّهِ the first *saakin* is from amongst the 'letters of *madd*', then the 'letter of *madd*' will be omitted in recitation.

Example: The phrase فِي الْأَرْضِ [البقرة:29], will be recited as فِ الْأَرْضِ , notice the *yaa* has been dropped.

(4) If in اِجْتِمَاعُ السَّاكِنَيْنِ عَلَى غَيْرِ حَدِّهِ the first *saakin* is **not** from amongst the 'letters of *madd*' then the first of the two *saakin's* will be given a **temporary harakah**. The temporary *harakah* given **will always be a *kasrah*** except in the following situations:

- If the first *saakin* is a 'plural *meem*' then it will be given a *dhammah*.

  Example: عَلَيْكُمُ الْقِصَاصُ [البقرة:178], in this phrase the 'plural *meem*' at the end of the word عَلَيْكُمْ is given a *dhammah* when continuing the recitation.

- If the first *saakin* is a *noon* of the preposition ( مِنْ ) or it is the *meem* of the word الم, then it will be given a *fathah*.

  Example: مِنَ اللهِ [آل عمران:159], in this phrase the *noon* at the end of the word مِنْ is given a *fathah* when continuing the recitation.

**Notes**:

(1) The phrase بِئْسَ الِاسْمُ [الحجرات:11] will be recited as بِئْسَ لِسْمُ in continuous recitation due to the rules mentioned above.

The *hamzah* prior to the letter *seen* in the word اسْمُ is a 'joining *hamzah*' which is dropped in continuous recitation. This results in the letter *seen* being the first letter which is a *saakin*. Also, the letter *laam* was a *saakin;* according to the rules mentioned above when two *saakin's* appear next to each other and the first is **not** from the 'letters of *madd*', then it will be given a *kasrah*. This is exactly what has occurred in بِئْسَ لِسْمُ .

(2) In the word كَأَيِّنْ [آل عمران:146], the *noon* that appears is really the '*noon* of *tanween*'; according to the rules of *tanween* when doing *waqf* upon this, the *noon* should be omitted in recitation. However, this is an exceptional case where the *noon* will be recited with a *saakin* when doing *waqf* as generally the writing and script is followed in the rules of *waqf*.

# Arabic Letters

There are 28 Arabic letters; some referring to them as 29 letters. The letter (ء) in some dictionaries is mentioned separately, whereas in most dictionaries it is mentioned within the letter (ا). However, as the two letters have different 'qualities' in terms of the *tajweed* rules, throughout the *tajweed* rules they have been treated separately.

The Arabic letters are written in two different orders;

- The 'Abjad order' (أَبْجَدِيّ)
- The 'Hija'i order' (هِجَائِيّ), this is also referred to 'Alphabetical order' (أَلِفْبَائِيّ)

# Abjad order

The 'Abjad order' was an order of the Arabic alphabet based on the assignment of a numerical value to each letter. This would aid in the remembrance of long words and sentences with small numerical figures. This system has been in existence within the Arabic speaking world since before the 8th century. There are a few variants that the 'Abjad order' was placed according to, however, below the most famous order will be mentioned.

|    | Letter | Value |    | Letter | Value |    | Letter | Value |
|----|--------|-------|----|--------|-------|----|--------|-------|
| 1  | ا      | 1     | 11 | ك      | 20    | 19 | ق      | 100   |
| 2  | ب      | 2     | 12 | ل      | 30    | 20 | ر      | 200   |
| 3  | ج      | 3     | 13 | م      | 40    | 21 | ش      | 300   |
| 4  | د      | 4     | 14 | ن      | 50    | 22 | ت      | 400   |
| 5  | ه      | 5     | 15 | س      | 60    | 23 | ث      | 500   |
| 6  | و      | 6     | 16 | ع      | 70    | 24 | خ      | 600   |
| 7  | ز      | 7     | 17 | ف      | 80    | 25 | ذ      | 700   |
| 8  | ح      | 8     | 18 | ص      | 90    | 26 | ض      | 800   |
| 9  | ط      | 9     |    |        |       | 27 | ظ      | 900   |
| 10 | ي      | 10    |    |        |       | 28 | غ      | 1000  |

**Example**: The following examples will demonstrate the use of 'Abjad numerals':

(1) The phrase بسم الله الرحمن الرحيم is referred to by the numeric value of 786.

| م | ي | ح | ر | ل | ا | ن | م | ح | ر | ل | ا | ه | ل | ل | ا | م | س | ب |
|---|---|---|---|---|---|---|---|---|---|---|---|---|---|---|---|---|---|---|
|40|10|8|200|30|1|50|40|8|200|30|1|5|30|30|1|40|60|2|

2+60+40+1+30+30+5+1+30+200+8+40+50+1+30+200+8+10+40=786

**Notes**: The 'Abjad order' letters can be remembered with the mnemonic

أَبْجَدْ هَوَّزْ حُطِّي كَلِمَنْ سَعْفَصْ قَرَشَتْ ثَخَذْ ضَظَغْ

In this mnemonic the first three words, namely أَبْجَدْ هَوَّزْ حُطِّي represent the unit numbers from 1-10 in order. The fourth and fifth words, namely كَلِمَنْ سَعْفَصْ represent the ten numbers from 20-90. The final three words, namely قَرَشَتْ ثَخَذْ ضَظَغْ represent the hundred (& thousand) numbers from 100-1000.

# Hija'i order

The 'Hija'i order' is the modern order of the Arabic alphabet based on the similarity of the shape of the letters. There are a few variants that the 'Hija'i order' was placed according to, however, below the most famous order will be mentioned.

|  | Letter | English Pronunciation | English translation |
|---|---|---|---|
| 1 | ا | Alif | ā / ' |
| 2 | ب | bā' | b |
| 3 | ت | tā' | t |
| 4 | ث | thā' | th |
| 5 | ج | Jīm | j |
| 6 | ح | ḥā' | ḥ |
| 7 | خ | khā' | kh |
| 8 | د | Dāl | d |
| 9 | ذ | Dhāl | dh |
| 10 | ر | rā' | r |
| 11 | ز | zayn/zāy | z |
| 12 | س | Sīn | s |
| 13 | ش | Shīn | sh |
| 14 | ص | ṣād | ṣ |
| 15 | ض | ḍād | ḍ |
| 16 | ط | ṭā' | ṭ |
| 17 | ظ | ẓā' | ẓ |
| 18 | ع | 'ayn | ' |
| 19 | غ | ghayn | gh |
| 20 | ف | fā' | f |
| 21 | ق | Qāf | q |
| 22 | ك | Kāf | k |
| 23 | ل | Lām | l |
| 24 | م | Mīm | m |
| 25 | ن | Nūn | n |
| 26 | ه | hā' | h |
| 27 | و | Wāw | w / ū |
| 28 | ء | a | a |
| 29 | ي | yā' | y / ī |

**Notes**: Most modern Arabic dictionaries use the order mentioned above, few Moroccan scripts have used a slightly different order for the *hija'i* alphabet. In Persian dictionaries the letter (و) appears before the letter (ه).

# Written transmission of the Qur'an

The Qur'an was committed to memory by the Prophet and his Companions; some memorising certain portions, whereas others memorising all revealed portions. The tradition of oral transmission continued beyond the Companions until modern era. However, coupled with this method of transmission, many individuals preserved the Qur'an in written text as well. This was again, ordered by the Prophet, himself to certain Companions. The transmission of the written text of the Qur'an in the different stages is indicated in the table below with an indication to the Era of the stage.

| Year (AD) (approximately) | Stage | Era |
|---|---|---|
| 610 | 1st revelation in the cave of Hira | Prophetic |
|  | Orally, later recorded in written text. ||
| 610-622 | Continuous revelation during Meccan period | Prophetic |
|  | Orally transmitted, also, certain Companions ordered to preserve in written text. ||
| 622-632 | Continuous revelation during Madinan period | Prophetic |
|  | Orally transmitted, also, certain companions ordered to preserve in written text. ||
| 632 | Last revelations before the demise of the Prophet | Prophetic |
|  | The full Qur'an preserved orally by some Companions and also present in written text by some Companions in individual isolated sheets. ||
| 632-34 | *Suhuf* remain with *Abu Bakr* | Abu Bakr |
|  | After the martyrdom of 70 Companions who had committed the Qur'an to memory in the battle of *Yamamah* (Dec 632AD), *Umar* requested *Abu Bakr* to compile a single written copy of the Qur'an, after earlier denial *Abu Bakr* agreed and ordered *Zaid bin Thabit* to compile a single copy in written format. *Zaid* compiled the Qur'an by asking for any written or oral preserved texts amongst the Companions, demanding two witnesses for each verse. This copy was referred to as *suhuf* (sheets). ||

| | | |
|---|---|---|
| 634-44 | *Suhuf* remain with *Umar* | *Umar* |
| | No changes made. *Suhuf* are passed from *Umar* to his daughter, the wife of the Prophet, *Hafsah*. | |
| 644-56 | *Mushaf* made under the instruction of *Uthman* | *Uthman* |
| | After returning from the battle against *Armenia* and *Azerbaijan* (653AD), where *Huzaifah bin Yamaan* witnessed the disagreements amongst Muslims due to the different modes of recitation, he requested *Uthman* to make copies of the *Suhuf* stored by *Hafsah* and send to the Muslim governors. Six copies were made, one sent to Kufa, one to Damascus, one to Basra, one to Makkah, one to Bahrain and one was left in Madinah with *Uthman*. The copy of *Hafsah* was returned to her. The governors were ordered to burn all other material of the Qur'an that was in circulation.<br>Within this era, the division of the Qur'an into 30 *juz* (parts) took place. This division was not based on meaning; instead they were equally divided 30 parts for the easiness of the readers. | |
| 656-661 | Dots appear in the Qur'an | *Ali* |
| | According to some reports, *Ali* ordered the grammarian *Abu al-Aswad al-Duwali* (d.69AH/688AD) to insert dots in the Qur'an when seeing the faltering in the recitation, especially within the non-Arabs. He placed dots in the Qur'an which symbolised the sound of the letters which is in modern times referred to as the *harakaat*. | |
| 661-750<br>750-786 | *Harakaat* appear in the Qur'an | *Umayyad Caliphate* (661AD-750AD)<br>*Abbasid Caliphate* (750AD-1258AD) |
| | According to some reports, the grammarian *Khalil bin Ahmed al-Farahidi* (b.718AD/100AH, d.786AD/170AH), invented the current standard for *harakaat* (vowel marks). The system that he invented, originally intended for poetry was much simpler than the previous systems of letters; hence, eventually his system was adopted within the Qura'nic script. In his symbols, he added applications for the *sukoon*, *mushaddad* and *madd*. Some have, loosely mentioned that *Hajjaj bin Yusuf* (b.660AD/40AH, d.714AD/660AH), ordered certain individuals to replace the dots symbolising sounds with the *harakaat* we see in the modern scripts; this includes the present day *fathah*, *kasrah* and *dhammah*. | |

And Allah knows best regarding the written transmission and stages of the Qura'nic text. Verily, he himself has said 'We have revealed the remembrance [the Qur'an] and it is us who safeguard it' (*Al-Hijr:* Verse 9).

# Chapters of the Qur'an

Below the 114 chapters of the Qur'an are mentioned in a table form, indicating the number of verses within each chapter and the period of revelation.

Most scholars have suggested the chapters of the *Qur'an* were divinely named.

| No. | Surah name (Arabic) | Surah name (English) | Meaning | Period of revelation | Number of verses |
|---|---|---|---|---|---|
| 1 | الفاتحة | Al-Fatihah | The Opening | Meccan | 7 |
| 2 | البقرة | Al-Baqarah | The Cow | Madinan | 286 |
| 3 | آل عمران | Al-'Imran | The Progeny of Imran | Madinan | 200 |
| 4 | النساء | An-Nisa' | The Women | Madinan | 176 |
| 5 | المائدة | Al-Ma'idah | The Table spread | Madinan | 120 |
| 6 | الأنعام | Al-An'am | The Cattle | Meccan | 165 |
| 7 | الأعراف | Al-A'raf | The Heights | Meccan | 206 |
| 8 | الأنفال | Al-Anfal | The Spoils of War | Madinan | 75 |
| 9 | التوبة (البراءة) | At-Tawbah | The Repentance | Madinan | 129 |
| 10 | يونس | Yunus | Jonah | Meccan | 109 |
| 11 | هود | Hud | Hud | Meccan | 123 |
| 12 | يوسف | Yusuf | Joseph | Meccan | 111 |
| 13 | الرعد | Ar-Ra'd | The Thunder | Meccan | 43 |
| 14 | إبراهيم | Ibrahim | Abraham | Meccan | 52 |
| 15 | الحجر | Al-Hijr | Al-Hijr | Meccan | 99 |
| 16 | النحل | An-Nahl | The Honey Bee | Meccan | 128 |
| 17 | بنو إسرائيل (الإسراء) | Bani Israel | Children of Israel | Meccan | 11 |
| 18 | الكهف | Al-Kahf | The Cave | Meccan | 110 |
| 19 | مريم | Maryam | Mary | Meccan | 98 |
| 20 | طه | Ta Ha | Ta-Ha | Meccan | 135 |
| 21 | الأنبياء | Al-Anbiya' | The Prophets | Meccan | 112 |
| 22 | الحج | Al-Hajj | The Pilgrimage | Madinan | 78 |
| 23 | المؤمنون | Al-Mu'minun | The Believers | Meccan | 118 |
| 24 | النور | An-Nur | The Light | Madinan | 64 |
| 25 | الفرقان | Al-Furqan | The Criterion | Meccan | 77 |
| 26 | الشعراء | Ash-Shu'ara' | The Poets | Meccan | 227 |
| 27 | النمل | An-Naml | The Ant | Meccan | 93 |

| 28 | القصص | *Al-Qasas* | The Stories | Meccan | 88 |
| --- | --- | --- | --- | --- | --- |
| 29 | العنكبوت | *Al-Ankabut* | The Spider | Meccan | 69 |
| 30 | الروم | *Ar-Rum* | The Romans | Meccan | 60 |
| 31 | لقمان | *Luqman* | Luqman | Meccan | 34 |
| 32 | السجدة | *As-Sajdah* | The Prostration | Meccan | 30 |
| 33 | الأحزاب | *Al-Ahzab* | The Coalition | Madinan | 73 |
| 34 | سبأ | *Saba'* | Sheba | Meccan | 54 |
| 35 | فاطر | *Al-Fatir* | The Originator | Meccan | 45 |
| 36 | يس | *Ya Seen* | Ya-Seen | Meccan | 83 |
| 37 | الصافّات | *As-Saffat* | Those Standing in Rows | Meccan | 182 |
| 38 | ص | *Saad* | Saad | Meccan | 88 |
| 39 | الزمر | *Az-Zumar* | The groups | Meccan | 75 |
| 40 | المؤمن (الغافر) | *Al-Mu'min* | The Believer | Meccan | 85 |
| 41 | فصّلت (حم سجدة) | *Fussilat* | Explained | Meccan | 54 |
| 42 | الشورى | *Ash-Shura* | The Counsel | Meccan | 53 |
| 43 | الزخرف | *Az-Zukhruf* | The Ornaments of Gold | Meccan | 89 |
| 44 | الدخان | *Ad-Dukhan* | The Smoke | Meccan | 59 |
| 45 | الجاثية | *Al-Jathiya* | The Kneeling | Meccan | 37 |
| 46 | الأحقاف | *Al-Ahqaf* | The Sand Dunes | Meccan | 35 |
| 47 | محمّد | *Muhammad* | Muhammad | Madinan | 38 |
| 48 | الفتح | *Al-Fath* | The Victory | Madinan | 29 |
| 49 | الحجرات | *Al-Hujurat* | The Chambers | Madinan | 18 |
| 50 | ق | *Qaf* | Qaf | Meccan | 45 |
| 51 | الذاريات | *Adh-Dhariyat* | The Scattering Winds | Meccan | 60 |
| 52 | الطور | *At-Tur* | The Mount of Tur | Meccan | 49 |
| 53 | النجم | *An-Najm* | The Star | Meccan | 62 |
| 54 | القمر | *Al-Qamar* | The Moon | Meccan | 55 |
| 55 | الرحمن | *Ar-Rahman* | The All Merciful | Madinan | 78 |
| 56 | الواقعة | *Al-Waqi'ah* | The Event | Meccan | 96 |
| 57 | الحديد | *Al-Hadid* | The Iron | Madinan | 29 |
| 58 | المجادلة | *Al-Mujadalah* | The Debate | Madinan | 22 |
| 59 | الحشر | *Al-Hashr* | The Gathering | Madinan | 24 |
| 60 | الممتحنة | *Al-Mumtahinah* | The Examiner | Madinan | 13 |
| 61 | الصفّ | *As-Saff* | The Ranks | Madinan | 14 |
| 62 | الجمعة | *Al-Jum'ah* | The Congregation | Madinan | 11 |

| 63 | المنافقون | Al-Munafiqun | The Hypocrites | Madinan | 11 |
| 64 | التغابن | At-Taghabun | The Loss & Gain | Madinan | 18 |
| 65 | الطلاق | At-Talaq | The Divorce | Madinan | 12 |
| 66 | التحريم | At-Tahrim | The Banning | Madinan | 12 |
| 67 | الملك | Al-Mulk | The Kingdom | Meccan | 30 |
| 68 | القلم (نون) | Al-Qalam | The Pen | Meccan | 52 |
| 69 | الحاقّة | Al-Haqqah | The Reality | Meccan | 52 |
| 70 | المعارج | Al-Ma'arij | The Stairways | Meccan | 44 |
| 71 | نوح | Nuh | Noah | Meccan | 28 |
| 72 | الجنّ | Al-Jinn | The Jinn | Meccan | 28 |
| 73 | المزّمّل | Al-Muzzammil | The Wrapped One | Meccan | 20 |
| 74 | المدّثّر | Al-Muddathir | The Cloaked One | Meccan | 56 |
| 75 | القيامة | Al-Qiyamah | The Resurrection | Meccan | 40 |
| 76 | الإنسان (الدهر) | Al-Insan | The Human Being | Meccan | 31 |
| 77 | المرسلات | Al-Mursalat | The Emissaries | Meccan | 50 |
| 78 | النبأ | An-Naba | The Great Event | Meccan | 40 |
| 79 | النازعات | An-Nazi'at | Those who Pull Out | Meccan | 46 |
| 80 | عبس | 'Abasa | He Frowned | Meccan | 42 |
| 81 | التكوير | At-Takwir | The folding | Meccan | 29 |
| 82 | الانفطار | Al-Infitar | The Splitting | Meccan | 19 |
| 83 | المطفّفين | Al-Muttaffifin | The Defrauding | Meccan | 36 |
| 84 | الانشقاق | Al-Inshiqaq | The Sundering | Meccan | 25 |
| 85 | البروج | Al-Buruj | The Milky Way | Meccan | 22 |
| 86 | الطارق | At-Tariq | The Night star | Meccan | 17 |
| 87 | الأعلى | Al-A'la | The Most High | Meccan | 19 |
| 88 | الغاشية | Al-Ghashiyah | The Overwhelming Event | Meccan | 26 |
| 89 | الفجر | Al-Fajr | The Dawn | Meccan | 30 |
| 90 | البلد | Al-Balad | The City | Meccan | 20 |
| 91 | الشمس | Ash-Shams | The Sun | Meccan | 15 |
| 92 | الليل | Al-Layl | The Night | Meccan | 21 |
| 93 | الضحى | Ad-Duha | The Forenoon | Meccan | 11 |
| 94 | الشرح | Ash-Sharh | The Solace | Meccan | 8 |
| 95 | التين | At-Tin | The Fig | Meccan | 8 |
| 96 | العلق | Al-'Alaq | The Clot | Meccan | 19 |
| 97 | القدر | Al-Qadr | The Power | Meccan | 5 |

| 98 | البيّنة | Al-Bayyinah | The Clear Proof | Madinan | 8 |
|---|---|---|---|---|---|
| 99 | الزلزلة | Al-Zalzalah | The Earthquake | Madinan | 8 |
| 100 | العاديات | Al-'Adiyat | The Chargers | Meccan | 11 |
| 101 | القارعة | Al-Qari'ah | The Striking Event | Meccan | 11 |
| 102 | التكاثر | At-Takathur | The Competition in Amassing | Meccan | 8 |
| 103 | العصر | Al-'Asr | The Time | Meccan | 3 |
| 104 | الهمزة | Al-Humazah | The Backbiter | Meccan | 9 |
| 105 | الفيل | Al-Fil | The Elephant | Meccan | 5 |
| 106 | قريش | Quraysh | Quraysh | Meccan | 4 |
| 107 | الماعون | Al-Ma'un | The Small Gifts | Meccan | 7 |
| 108 | الكوثر | Al-Kawthar | The Kawthar | Meccan | 3 |
| 109 | الكافرون | Al-Kafirun | The Disbelievers | Meccan | 6 |
| 110 | النصر | An-Nasr | The Help | Madinan | 3 |
| 111 | المسد (اللهب) | Al-Masad | The Flame | Meccan | 5 |
| 112 | الإخلاص | Al-Ikhlas | The Sincerity | Meccan | 4 |
| 113 | الفلق | Al-Falaq | The Break of Dawn | Meccan | 5 |
| 114 | الناس | An-Nas | The Mankind | Meccan | 6 |

Scholars have differed in terms of the order of the revelation of the chapters *(surahs)* of the Qur'an. One scholar who has indicated to an order of revelation is *al-Nadim* in his book *fihrist*, he has placed the *surahs* in the following order of revelation (the numbers used are according to the *surah* numbers mentioned above):

'96, 68, 73, 74, 111, 81, 87, 94, 103, 89, 93, 92, 100, 108, 102, 107, 114, 53, 80, 97, 91, 85, 95, 106, 101, 75, 104, 77, 50, 90, 55, 72, 36, 25, 35, 19, 20, 56, 26, 27, 28, 17, 11, 12, 10, 15, 37, 31, 23, 34, 21, 39, 40, 41, 42, 43, 44, 45, 46, 51, 88, 18, 6, 16, 71, 14, 32, 52, 67, 69, 70, 78, 79, 82, 84, 30, 29, 83, 54, 86, 2, 8, 7, 3, 60, 4, 99, 57, 47, 13, 76, 65, 98, 59, 110, 24, 22, 63, 58, 49, 66, 62, 64, 61, 48, 5, 9'

However, as indicated above, there has been some disagreement amongst scholars regarding the order of certain chapters in terms of revelation.

# The Different Qira'ah

The easiness of the Qur'an is not restricted to memorisation, etc. Instead, for the different accents, different civilisations, the recitation was made easy by allowing them to pray according to their dialect. Despite the majority of the Muslim world reciting upon the recitation of Imam *Hafs al-Asadi* who is a transmitter from *'Aasim al-Kufi*; in total there were many more methods of recitation, some authentic and others lacking in authenticity. Scholars have agreed upon the authenticity of seven different forms of Qira'ah, and the majority of scholars have agreed upon the authenticity of an additional three forms of Qira'ah; in total there are ten authentic forms of Qira'ah. The reciters and their transmitters are indicated in the tables below. The forms of recitation which are external to these ten are regarded as unauthentic, and hence not valid to pray in Salaah.

The *tajweed* rules in this book are generally based upon the recitation of **Hafs al-Asadi** who is transmitter from **'Aasim al-Kufi**, occasionally other modes of recitation are indicated to.

*Hafs al-Asadi* has the agnomen *Abu 'Amr* and his full name is *Hafs bin Sulaiman bin al-Mugeerah al-Asadi*, commonly known as the Qari (reciter) of Kufah. He also descended in Baghdad and took residence close to Makkah. He was the most knowledgeable regarding the recitation of *'Asim al-Kufi* who was also his stepfather.

Generally, throughout the world the transmission of *Hafs al-Asadi* is read; however, some other forms are also prevalent in certain areas of the modern world. These are indicated in the table below.

|   | Qari (reciter) | Rawi (transmitter) | Region of the world where it is read |
|---|---|---|---|
| 1 | Nafi' al-Madani | Qalun | Libya<br>Tunisia<br>Parts of al-Andalus<br>Parts of Qatar |
| 2 | | Warsh | Al-Andalus<br>Algeria<br>Morocco<br>Parts of Tunisia<br>West Africa<br>Sudan<br>Parts of Libya |
| 3 | Abu 'Amr ibn al-'Ala | Hafs al-Duri | Parts of Sudan<br>West Africa |
| 4 | Ibn 'Amir al-Dimishqi | Hisham | Parts of Yemen |
| 5 | 'Aasim al-Kufi | Hafs al-Asadi | Most of the Muslim world |

| | Qari (Reader) | | | | Rawi (Transmitter) | | | |
|---|---|---|---|---|---|---|---|---|
| | Name | Born | Died | Place | Name | Born | Died | Place |
| 1 | Nafi' al-Madani | 70AH 690AD | 169AH 785AD | Madinah | *Qalun* (Prayed to *Nafi'* in 150AH) | 120AH 738AD | 220AH 835AD | Madinah |
| | | | | | *Warsh* (Prayed to *Nafi'* in 155AH) | 110AH 728AD | 197AH 812AD | Egypt |
| 2 | Ibn Katheer al-Makki | 45AH 665AD | 120AH 738AD | Makkah | *Al-Buzzi* (There are two transmitters between him and Ibn Katheer) | 170AH 786AD | 250AH 864AD | Makkah |
| | | | | | *Qunbul* (There are four transmitters between him and Ibn Katheer) | 195AH 810AD | 291AH 904AD | Makkah |
| 3 | Abu 'Amr ibn al-'Ala | 70AH 690AD | 154AH 771AD | Basrah | *Hafs al-Duri* | 150AH 767AD | 246AH 860AD | Baghdad |
| | | | | | *Al-Susi* | | 261AH 875AD | Iran |
| 4 | Ibn 'Amir al-Dimishqi | 8AH 630AD | 118AH 736AD | Damascus | *Hisham* (There are two transmitters between him and Ibn 'Amir) | 153AH 770AD | 245AH 859AD | Damascus |
| | | | | | *Ibn Dhakwan* (There are two transmitters between him and Ibn 'Amir) | 173AH 789AD | 242AH 856AD | Damascus |
| 5 | 'Aasim al-Kufi | | 127AH 745AD | Kufah | *Shu'bah* (Prayed to *'Aasim* many times) | 95AH 714AD | 193AH 809AD | Kufah |
| | | | | | *Hafs al-Asadi* (Prayed to *'Aasim* many times) | 90AH 709AD | 180AH 796AD | Kufah |

| | | | | | | | |
|---|---|---|---|---|---|---|---|
| 6 | Hamzah al-Kufi al-Taymi | 80AH 700AD | 156AH 773AD | Kufah | Khalaf al-Asadi (There is one transmitter between him and Hamzah) | 150AH 767AD | 229AH 844AD | Baghdad |
| | | | | | Khallad (There is one transmitter between him and Hamzah) | 130AH 748AD | 220AH 835AD | Kufah |
| 7 | Al-Kisa'i al-Kufi al-Asadi | | 189AH 805AD | Kufah | Abu al-Harith Al-Layth (Prayed directly from Al-Kisa'i) | | 240AH 854AD | Baghdad |
| | | | | | Hafs al-Duri (Prayed directly from Al-Kisa'i) | 150AH 767AD | 246AH 860AD | Baghdad |
| 8 | Abu Ja'far al-Madani | | 130AH 748AD | Madinah | 'Isa Ibn Wirdan (Prayed directly from Abu Ja'far) | | 160AH 776AD | Madinah |
| | | | | | Sulaiman bin Jummaz (Prayed directly from Abu Ja'far) | | after 170AH 786AD | Madinah |
| 9 | Ya'qub al-Hadhrami al-Basri | 117AH 735AD | 205AH 821AD | Basrah | Ruways (Prayed directly from Ya'qub) | | 238AH 853AD | Basrah |
| | | | | | Rawh (Prayed directly from Ya'qub) | | 234/235AH 849/850AD | Basrah |
| 10 | Khalaf al-Asadi | 150AH 767AD | 229AH 844AD | Baghdad | Ishaq al-Warraq (Prayed directly from Khalaf) | | 286AH 899AD | Baghdad |
| | | | | | Idris al-Haddad (Prayed directly from Khalaf) | | 292AH 905AD | Baghdad |

# Recitation according to *Hafs al-Asadi*

The script of the Qur'an is written such that it agrees with all of the 7 different codes of recitation. Therefore, there are some places within the Qur'an where the recitation for the readers could get confusing. These places are noted below with the method of recitation according to *Hafs al-Asadi*.

## The letter (ص) or (س):

There are 4 places within the Qur'an where the different scholars of recitation have differed in terms of reciting the letter (س) in those places or the letter (ص).

|   | Word | What does *Hafs* pray? |
|---|------|------------------------|
| 1 | يَبْصُۜطُ (البقرة:245) | س |
| 2 | بَصْۜطَةً (الأعراف:69) | س |
| 3 | الْمُصَۜيْطِرُونَ (الطّور:37) | (س)(ص) |
| 4 | بِمُصَۜيْطِرٍ (الغاشية:22) | (ص) |

Few other important rules for *Hafs* recitation:

|   | Word | How does *Hafs* pray? |
|---|------|------------------------|
| 1 | مَجْرٰىهَا (هود:41) | *Hafs* prays the *raa* and the *alif* (after it) with إمالة. That is praying the *raa* and *alif* inbetween a *fathah-kasrah* and *alif-yaa* combination. |
| 2 | لَا تَأْمَنَّا (يوسف:11) | *Hafs* prays the *noon* with إشمام, which is indicating with the lips after praying the *meem* towards a *dhammah*, thereafter, continue by praying the *noon* in the normal method. |
| 3 | ءَاَعْجَمِيٌّ (فصّلت:44) | *Hafs* prays the second *hamzah* with تسهيل, which is praying the alif inbetween a *alif-haa* combination. The first *alif* will be pronounced as a normal *alif*. |

| | | |
|---|---|---|
| 4 | ضُعْفٍ <br> (الروم:54) | This word occurs three times within the same verse, in all three words *Hafs* allows the recitation of the letter (ض) with a *dhammah* or a *fathah*; however, the preferred option is *dhammah*. |
| 5 | لَٰكِنَّا۠ <br> (الكهف:38) | When continuing the recitation the *alif* at the end of the word will **not** be recited; however, when pausing upon the word, the *alif* will be read. |
| 6 | الظُّنُونَا۠ <br> (الأحزاب:10) | |
| 7 | الرَّسُولَا۠ <br> (الأحزاب:66) | |
| 8 | السَّبِيلَا۠ <br> (الأحزاب:67) | |
| 9 | أَنَا۠ <br> (الأعراف:12 وص:76) | |
| 10 | قَوَارِيرَا۠ <br> (الإنسان:15) | This word appears at the end of Ayah 15 in *surah al-Insan*. When continuing the recitation the *alif* at the end of the word will **not** be recited; however, when pausing upon the word, the *alif* will be read. |
| 11 | قَوَارِيرَا۠ <br> (الإنسان:16) | This word appears at the beginning of Ayah 16 in *surah al-Insan*. When continuing the recitation or pausing, the *alif* at the end of the word will **not** be recited according to the recitation of *Hafs*. |
| 12 | سَلَاسِلَا۠ <br> (الإنسان:4) | When continuing the recitation the *alif* at the end of the word will **not** be recited; however, when pausing upon the word, it is optional to recite the *alif* or to drop the *alif* in recitation. |
| 13 | فَمَا آتَىٰنِ <br> (النمل:36) | When continuing the recitation the *yaa* at the end of the word will be recited; however, when pausing upon the word, it is optional to pause upon the *yaa* or to drop the *yaa* in recitation and pause upon the *noon*. |
| 14 | بَسَطتَّ <br> (المائدة:28) | When reciting this word, the letter ط will be completely merged within the letter ت ; the recitation will be of two ت . However, the quality of إطباق within the letter ط will remain; it will not be changed to انفتاح . |

# Broken letters – حروف مقطّعات

There are 29 chapters within the Qur'an from amongst the 114 chapters that begin with a letter or a few letters that are not read according to the normal method of pronunciation; instead these letters are all read separately. These letters are called حروف مقطّعات (broken letters). Some rules regarding these letters were discussed throughout the book.

In this chapter, the 14 different حروف مقطّعات that are at the beginning of the 29 chapters are mentioned with their method of pronunciation. Thereafter, the chapters they occur at the beginning of will be mentioned.

|    | Broken letters | Pronunciation method |
|----|----------------|----------------------|
| 1  | الٓمٓ           | اَلِفْ لَآمْ مِّيْمْ |
| 2  | الٓمٓصٓ         | اَلِفْ لَآمْ مِّيْمْ صَآدْ |
| 3  | الٓرٰ           | اَلِفْ لَآمْ رَا |
| 4  | الٓمٓرٰ         | اَلِفْ لَآمْ مِيْمْ رَا |
| 5  | كٓهٰيٰعٓصٓ      | كَآفْ هَا يَا عَيْنْ صَآدْ |
| 6  | طٰهٰ            | طَاهَا |
| 7  | طٰسٓمٓ          | طَاسِيْمْ مِّيْمْ |
| 8  | طٰسٓ            | طَاسِيْنْ |
| 9  | يٰسٓ            | يَاسِيْنْ |
| 10 | صٓ              | صَآدْ |
| 11 | حٰمٓ            | حَامِيْمْ |
| 12 | حٰمٓ عٓسٓقٓ     | حَامِيْمْ عَيْنْ سِيْنْ قَآفْ |
| 13 | قٓ              | قَآفْ |
| 14 | نٓ              | نُوْنْ |

138

| | | | | الٓمٓ | | |
|---|---|---|---|---|---|---|
| Surah Name | البقرة<br>Al-Baqarah | آل عمران<br>Al-'Imran | العنكبوت<br>Al-Ankabut | الروم<br>Ar-Rum | لقمان<br>Luqman | السجدة<br>As-Sajdah |
| Surah Number | 2 | 3 | 29 | 30 | 31 | 32 |

| | الٓمٓصٓ | | الٓر | | | |
|---|---|---|---|---|---|---|
| Surah Name | الأعراف<br>Al-A'raf | يونس<br>Yunus | هود<br>Hud | يوسف<br>Yusuf | إبراهيم<br>Ibrahim | الحجر<br>Al-Hijr |
| Surah Number | 7 | 10 | 11 | 12 | 14 | 15 |

| | الٓمٓر | كٓهيعٓصٓ | طه | طسٓمٓ | | طسٓ |
|---|---|---|---|---|---|---|
| Surah Name | الرعد<br>Ar-Ra'd | مريم<br>Maryam | طه<br>Ta Ha | الشعراء<br>Ash-Shu'ara' | القصص<br>Al-Qasas | النمل<br>An-Naml |
| Surah Number | 13 | 19 | 20 | 26 | 28 | 27 |

| | | | حمٓ | | | |
|---|---|---|---|---|---|---|
| Surah Name | المؤمن<br>Al-Mu'min | فصّلت<br>Fussilat | الزخرف<br>Az-Zukhruf | الدخان<br>Ad-Dukhan | الجاثية<br>Al-Jathiya | الأحقاف<br>Al-Ahqaf |
| Surah Number | 40 | 41 | 43 | 44 | 45 | 46 |

| | يسٓ | صٓ | حمٓ عٓسٓقٓ | قٓ | نٓ |
|---|---|---|---|---|---|
| Surah Name | يس<br>Ya Seen | ص<br>Saad | الشورى<br>Ash-Shura | ق<br>Qaf | القلم<br>Al-Qalam |
| Surah Number | 36 | 38 | 42 | 50 | 68 |

# Prostration Places within the Qur'an

There are certain places within the Qur'an where scholars have indicated to the good practice of prostrating after reciting those verses. In total, there are 15 places within the Qur'an where the prostration has been mentioned by scholars, below the places of prostration for the four famous schools of Jurisprudence are indicated. Also, indicating the verse number after which the prostration will be performed.

| No. | Para | Surah name | Surah number | Verse number | *Hanafi* School | *Maliki* School | *Shafe'e* School | *Hanbali* School |
|---|---|---|---|---|---|---|---|---|
| 1 | 9 | Al-A'raf | 7 | 206 | ✓ | ✓ | ✓ | ✓ |
| 2 | 13 | Ar-Ra'd | 13 | 15 | ✓ | ✓ | ✓ | ✓ |
| 3 | 14 | An-Nahl | 16 | 50 | ✓ | ✓ | ✓ | ✓ |
| 4 | 15 | Bani Israel | 17 | 109 | ✓ | ✓ | ✓ | ✓ |
| 5 | 16 | Maryam | 19 | 58 | ✓ | ✓ | ✓ | ✓ |
| 6 | 17 | Al-Hajj | 22 | 18 | ✓ | ✓ | ✓ | ✓ |
| 7 | 17 | Al-Hajj | 22 | 77 | ✗ | ✗ | ✓ | ✓ |
| 8 | 19 | Al-Furqan | 25 | 60 | ✓ | ✓ | ✓ | ✓ |
| 9 | 19 | An-Naml | 27 | 26 | ✓ | ✓ | ✓ | ✓ |
| 10 | 21 | As-Sajdah | 32 | 15 | ✓ | ✓ | ✓ | ✓ |
| 11 | 23 | Saad | 38 | 25 | ✓ | ✓ | ✗ | ✗ |
| 12 | 24 | Fussilat | 41 | 38 | ✓ | ✓ | ✓ | ✓ |
| 13 | 27 | An-Najm | 53 | 62 | ✓ | ✗ | ✓ | ✓ |
| 14 | 30 | Al-Inshiqaq | 84 | 21 | ✓ | ✗ | ✓ | ✓ |
| 15 | 30 | Al-'Alaq | 96 | 19 | ✓ | ✗ | ✓ | ✓ |

**Note**: The *Hanafi* and *Maliki* jurists have a slight difference regarding the prostration on *surah saad*; the *Hanafi* jurists prefer the prostration after the recitation of verse 25, whereas the *Maliki* jurists have preferred the prostration after the recitation of verse 24.

**Few rules concerning the prostration:**

(1) The prostration in the places mentioned above is Sunnah according to *Maliki, Shafe'e* and *Hanbali* scholars, the *Hanafi* scholars have mentioned it is Wajib.

(2) If the verse of prostration is repeated within the same gathering a few times then it is preferred to perform the prostration as many times according to *Maliki, Shafe'e* and *Hanbali* scholars, the *Hanafi* scholars mention prostrating once is enough. However, the *Maliki* scholars have added if the repetition is due to studying purposes then, similar to the *Hanafi* scholars, prostrating once will suffice.

(3) It is disliked for an Imam to read one of the verses of prostration in the prayers which are read quietly.

(4) The *muqtadi* (follower in *salaah*) should only perform the prostration in *salaah* if the *imam* performs the prostration.

(5) It is not compulsory to perform the prostration if the recitation was heard from a non-human source or from an individual who is not *mukallaf* (accountable).

**Method of prostration:**

(1) According to the *Hanafi* jurists the individual will pray the *takbeer* twice; one when going for prostration and one when coming up from prostration. These two *takbeer's* themselves are *Sunnah;* leaving them is disliked but will allow the completion of the prostration. Further, *tashahhud* or *salaam* is not performed with this prostration.

There is one main aspect of the prostration according to the *Hanafi* jurists; placing the forehead on the ground (or anything equivalent, like ruku, or indication by the ill, etc).

(2) According to the *Maliki* jurists the individual will pray the *takbeer* twice; one when going for prostration and one when coming up from prostration. These two *takbeer's* themselves are *Mustahab* (preferable); leaving them is disliked but will allow the completion of the prostration. Further, *tashahhud* or *salaam* is not performed with this prostration.

(3) According to the *Shafe'e* jurists the individual who is not in *salaah* will verbally (preferably) make intention for prostration, he will then perform the *takbeer* of commencing prayer (takbeer al-tahreemah) by lifting his hands, then he will do the *takbeer* for going into prostration, thereafter the *takbeer* for rising from prostration. Finally, he will sit and perform *salaam* after the prostration.

(4) According to the *Hanbali* jurists the individual will pray the *takbeer* twice; one when going for prostration and one when coming up from prostration. These two *takbeer's* are *wajib* according to them. Further, according to them it is important to do one *salaam* after the prostration. It is preferable to sit after performing the prostration whilst completing the *salaam*. *Tashahhud* is not read after the prostration.

## What should be read in the prostration?

Many supplications have been recorded for the prostration, they are:

سُبْحَانَ رَبِّيَ الْأَعْلَى [صحيح مسلم: ح1850] ثلاثا

**Translation**: Glory be to my Lord, Most High,

اللَّهُمَّ اكْتُبْ لِي بِهَا عِنْدَكَ أَجْرًا وَضَعْ عَنِّي بِهَا وِزْرًا وَاجْعَلْهَا لِي عِنْدَكَ ذُخْرًا وَتَقَبَّلْهَا مِنِّي كَمَا تَقَبَّلْتَهَا مِنْ عَبْدِكَ دَاوُدَ [سنن الترمذيّ: ح582]

**Translation**: O Allah! Record for me, a reward with You for it, remove a sin for me by it, and store it away for me with You, and accept it from me as You accepted it from Your worshipper *Dawud*.

سَجَدَ وَجْهِيَ لِلَّذِي خَلَقَهُ وَصَوَّرَهُ وَشَقَّ سَمْعَهُ وَبَصَرَهُ تَبَارَكَ اللَّهُ أَحْسَنُ الْخَالِقِينَ [صحيح مسلم: ح1848]

**Translation**: My face prostrates itself to Him Who created it and brought forth its hearing and seeing, blessed is Allah the best of Creators.

# Prophets mentioned in the Qur'an

From amongst the many Prophets sent to Mankind, the names of 25 Prophets have been mentioned within the Qur'an. The table below mentions their names:

| No. | Name | Transliteration | English name | Number of times mentioned by name |
|---|---|---|---|---|
| 1 | موسى | Musa | Moses | 136 |
| 2 | إبراهيم | Ibrahim | Abraham | 69 |
| 3 | نوح | Nuh | Noah | 43 |
| 4 | يوسف | Yusuf | Joseph | 27 |
| 5 | لوط | Lut | Lot | 27 |
| 6 | آدم | Adam | Adam | 25 |
| 7 | عيسى | Isa | Jesus | 25 |
| 8 | هارون | Harun | Aaron | 20 |
| 9 | سليمان | Sulaiman | Solomon | 17 |
| 10 | إسحاق | Ishaq | Isaac | 17 |
| 11 | داود | Dawud | David | 16 |
| 12 | يعقوب | Ya'qub | Jacob | 16 |
| 13 | إسماعيل | Isma'il | Ishmael | 12 |
| 14 | شعيب | Shu'aib | Shuaib | 11 |
| 15 | صالح | Saleh | Saleh | 9 |
| 16 | هود | Hud | Hud | 7 |
| 17 | زكريّا | Zakariya | Zachariah | 7 |
| 18 | يحيى | Yahya | John | 5 |
| 19 | محمّد أو أحمد | Muhammad or Ahmad | Muhammad or Ahmad | Muhammad:4 Ahmad:1 |
| 20 | أيوب | Ayyub | Job | 4 |
| 21 | يونس | Yunus | Jonah | 4 |
| 22 | إدريس | Idris | Idris | 2 |
| 23 | إلياس | Ilyas | Elias | 2 |
| 24 | ذو الكفل | Dhul-Kifl | Dhul-Kifl | 2 |
| 25 | اليسع | Al-Yasaa | Elisha | 2 |

# Information regarding the Qur'an

After discussing the rules of *tajweed* in detail it would be useful for the readers to learn some additional information regarding the Qur'an.

- The Qur'an is the final heavenly book to be revealed; in total, 114 heavenly books or scriptures were revealed, some have indicated to 104 being revealed and others have suggested 315 being revealed.

- However, none of the previous books have reached us in its entirety and authenticity. Hence, coupled with the revelation of the final heavenly book, namely the Qur'an, Allah has, himself, took the responsibility of preserving the exact wording of the Qur'an. He mentions;

إِنَّا نَحْنُ نَزَّلْنَا الذِّكْرَ وَإِنَّا لَهُ لَحَافِظُونَ [الحجر:9]

'We have revealed the remembrance [the Qur'an] and it is us who safeguard it' [Al-Hijr:9]

- The Qur'an was revealed approximately 600 years after the revelation of the previous heavenly book, namely *Injeel*. The final Prophet, *Muhammad*, himself was born approximately 6155 years after *Adam* عليه الصلاة والسلام, approximately 3913 years after the flood that came upon the nation of *Nuh* عليه السلام, approximately 2832 years after *Ibrahim* عليه الصلاة والسلام, approximately 2287 years after *Musa* عليه الصلاة والسلام and approximately 570 years after *Isa* عليه الصلاة والسلام.

- The Prophet *Muhammad* ﷺ was born on a Monday according to all scholars, also, he was born in the Islamic month of Rabi'ul Awwal according to all scholars, some have indicated this was the 8th of Rabi'ul Awwal, some have mentioned 9th and some have mentioned 12th.

- The Qur'an differs with Hadeeth (Prophetic sayings) in the sense that the Qur'an wording and meaning is from Allah, whereas in the Hadeeth, the meaning is from Allah but the wording is from the Prophet *Muhammad* ﷺ. Qur'an is referred to as الوحي المتلوّ (*al-Wahy al-Matloo*) and the Hadeeth is referred to as الوحي غير المتلوّ (*al-Wahy Gair al-Matloo*).

- The Qur'an consists of 7 sections (*hizb/manzil*). The Companions and Successors used to write a seventh of the Qur'an daily, completing the writing in a week; hence, the development of the seven sections (*ahzaab*). The seven sections are divided as follows:

| *Manzil* number | *Surah* included: |
|---|---|
| 1 | 1–4 |
| 2 | 5–9 |
| 3 | 10–16 |
| 4 | 17–25 |
| 5 | 26–36 |
| 6 | 37–49 |
| 7 | 50–114 |

- The Qur'an consists of 30 parts *(juz)*. This division is not based on meaning; instead they are equally divided 30 parts for the easiness of the readers.
- The Qur'an consists of 114 chapters *(surah* p.*suwar)*. *Surah* means high degree or steps for a structure; each *surah* is indeed of a high degree and a step for the overall structure of the Qur'an.
- The Qur'an consists of 558 paragraphs *(rukus)* (other views have been mentioned like 540 paragraphs). The *rukus* are indicated on the side of the Qur'an page by the letter (ع).
- There are approximately 6,136 verses *(ayahs)* within the Qur'an (other views have been mentioned including; 6000 verses, 6214 verses, 6219 verses, 6225 verses, 6226 verses and 6236 verses.). *Ayah* means sign; each *ayah* is indeed a sign and miracle upon the true nature of the religion, Allah and Prophethood of *Muhammed* ﷺ.
- There are approximately 77,934 words within the Qur'an (other views have been mentioned like 86,430 words).
- There are approximately 323,670 letters within the Qur'an (others views have been mentioned like 322,671 letters).
- There are approximately 1,025,030 dots within the Qur'an.
- There are approximately 53,243 *fathahs* within the Qur'an.
- There are approximately 39,582 *kasrahs* within the Qur'an.
- There are approximately 8,804 *dhammas* within the Qur'an.
- There are approximately 105,682 *saakins* within the Qur'an.
- There are approximately 1,253 *tashdeeds* within the Qur'an.
- There are approximately 771 *Madds* within the Qur'an.
- Originally the Qur'an was read without dots, *fathah, dhammah, kasrah, saakin, tashdeed, madd*. The dots were placed within the Qura'nic script by *Abu al-Aswad al-Duwali* (d.69AH/688CE). The *saakin, tashdeed* and *madd* were added to the Qura'nic script by *Khaleel bin Ahmad al-Basri*. The *fathah, dhammah* and *kasrah* were placed in the Qura'nic script by *Hajjaj bin Yusuf as-Saqafi*.
- The second chapter *Al-Baqarah* (The Cow) is the **longest** chapter within the Qur'an; it is approximately one-twelfth of the Qur'an.
- The hundred and twelfth chapter *Al-Ikhlas* (The Sincerity) is the **shortest** chapter within the Qur'an according to some, others suggest the hundred and eighth chapter *Al-Kawthar* (The Kawthar) is the **shortest** chapter within the Qur'an. *Al-Ikhlas* consists of four verses and *Al-Kawthar* consists of three verses.

- The Qur'an was **not** revealed upon the Prophet all at once, instead it was revealed over a span of time, some revealed during the Meccan period and some revealed during the Madinan period.
- The first revelation was during the month of Ramadhan, six months into the 41st year of the Prophet's life. Some scholars have reported the first revelation was on the night of 15th Ramadhan. This revelation took place in the cave of *Hira*. The first verses to be revealed were the first three (according to some scholars, first five) verses of surah *Al-'Alaq* (The Clot), the ninety sixth chapter of the Qur'an. The remaining verses of the surah were revealed at a later date.
- There are major differences amongst scholars regarding the last revelation. One of the latest revelations upon the Prophet (according to some scholars, this was the last revelation) was the verse:

الْيَوْمَ أَكْمَلْتُ لَكُمْ دِينَكُمْ وَأَتْمَمْتُ عَلَيْكُمْ نِعْمَتِي وَرَضِيتُ لَكُمُ الْإِسْلَامَ دِينًا [المائدة:3]

This is a portion of the third verse of the fifth chapter, namely, *Al-Ma'idah* (The Table spread). The revelation of this verse occurred on the 9th of *Dhul Hijjah* (the day of *Arafah*). This was during the 63rd year of the Prophet's life. This would suggest the time span between the first and last revelation was twenty-two years, two months and twenty-two days.

Most scholars have commented the last verse to be revealed was:

وَاتَّقُوا يَوْمًا تُرْجَعُونَ فِيهِ إِلَى اللَّهِ ثُمَّ تُوَفَّىٰ كُلُّ نَفْسٍ مَا كَسَبَتْ وَهُمْ لَا يُظْلَمُونَ [البقرة:281]

This is the two hundred and eighty first verse of the second chapter, namely, *Al-Baqarah* (The Cow). According to some scholars this verse was revealed 9 days prior to the demise of the Prophet.

Scholars have indicated the last *Surah* to be revealed in its complete form was the chapter of *An-Nasr* (The Help), this is the hundred and tenth chapter of the Qur'an.
- The Meccan period lasted twelve years, five months and thirteen days. The Madinan period lasted nine years, seven months and seven days. This would result in a total of twenty two years and twenty days. However, many scholars have indicated to a slightly longer time span that this, some have commented the time span between the first and last revelation was twenty-two years, two months and twenty-two days.
- The revelation of the Qur'an upon the Prophet *Muhammad* took different forms, they include:
    - Through dreams.
    - Tingling sound in *Muhammad's* ear.
    - Direct dialogue between Allah and *Muhammad*.

- Dialogue between Allah and *Muhammad* through *Jibraeel*, whilst *Jibraeel* was in his original angel form.
- Dialogue between Allah and *Muhammad* through *Jibraeel*, whilst *Jibraeel* was in human form.
- Dialogue between Allah and *Muhammad* through *Jibraeel*, whilst *Jibraeel* was in an invisible form.

**Note**: The transmissions through *Jibraeel* in human form or invisible form were the most common methods of revelation.

- Overall, the Qur'an took three journeys during its revelation upon *Muhammad*
    (1) The Qur'an in its entirety descended at once upon the seventh heaven, preserved within *Al-Lowhul Mahfooz*.
    (2) Thereafter, at a later date the Qur'an descended upon the nearest heaven, preserved within *Baitul Izzah* or *Al-Baitul Ma'moor*.
    (3) Finally, the revelation in isolated parts and verses upon the Prophet *Muhammad*.
- There were six famous teachers of the Qur'an from amongst the Companions, they are:
    - *Uthmaan bin Affan*.
    - *Ali bin Abi Talib*.
    - *Zaid bin Thabit*.
    - *Ubaiy ibn Ka'ab*.
    - *Abu Musa al-As'ari*.
    - *Abdullah bin Masood*.

# Virtues regarding the Qur'an

After discussing the rules of *tajweed* in detail it would be useful for the readers to learn some virtues regarding Qura'nic recitation. Verily, the virtues of recitation of the Qur'an are numerous, below a few narrations and sayings are indicated:

عَنِ النَّبِيِّ صلى الله عليه وسلم قَالَ: خَيْرُكُمْ مَنْ تَعَلَّمَ الْقُرْآنَ وَعَلَّمَهُ [صحيح البخاريّ]

The Messenger of Allah said: "The best amongst you is the one who learns the Qur'an and teaches it." [Sahih *al-Bukhari*]

عَنِ النَّبِيِّ صلى الله عليه وسلم قَالَ: لاَ حَسَدَ إِلاَّ عَلَى اثْنَتَيْنِ رَجُلٌ آتَاهُ اللَّهُ الْكِتَابَ وَقَامَ بِهِ آنَاءَ اللَّيْلِ وَرَجُلٌ أَعْطَاهُ اللَّهُ مَالاً فَهُوَ يَتَصَدَّقُ بِهِ آنَاءَ اللَّيْلِ وَالنَّهَارِ [صحيح البخاريّ]

The Messenger of Allah said: "Envy is not justified but in case of two persons only: one who, having been given (knowledge of) the Qur'an by Allah, recites it during the night and day (and also acts upon it) and a man who, having been given wealth by God, spends it during the night and the day (for the welfare of others, seeking the pleasure of the Lord)." [Sahih *al-Bukhari*]

عَنِ النَّبِيِّ صلى الله عليه وسلم قَالَ: الْمَاهِرُ بِالْقُرْآنِ مَعَ السَّفَرَةِ الْكِرَامِ الْبَرَرَةِ وَالَّذِى يَقْرَأُ الْقُرْآنَ وَيَتَتَعْتَعُ فِيهِ وَهُوَ عَلَيْهِ شَاقٌّ لَهُ أَجْرَانِ [صحيح مسلم]

The Messenger of Allah said: "One who is proficient in the Qur'an is associated with the noble, upright, recording angels; and he who falters in it, and finds it difficult for him, will have a double reward." [Sahih *al-Muslim*]

عَنِ النَّبِيِّ صلى الله عليه وسلم قَالَ: إِنَّ اللَّهَ يَرْفَعُ بِهَذَا الْكِتَابِ أَقْوَامًا وَيَضَعُ بِهِ آخَرِينَ [صحيح مسلم]

The Messenger of Allah said: "Verily, Allah elevates some people with this Qur'an and abases others." [Sahih *al-Muslim*]

عَنِ النَّبِيِّ صلى الله عليه وسلم قَالَ: إِنَّمَا مَثَلُ صَاحِبِ الْقُرْآنِ كَمَثَلِ صَاحِبِ الإِبِلِ الْمُعَقَّلَةِ إِنْ عَاهَدَ عَلَيْهَا أَمْسَكَهَا وَإِنْ أَطْلَقَهَا ذَهَبَتْ [صحيح البخاريّ]

The Messenger of Allah said: "The example of the person who knows the Qur'an by heart is like the owner of tied camels. If he keeps them tied, he will control them, but if he releases them, they will run away." [Sahih *al-Bukhari*]

عَنِ النَّبِيِّ صلى الله عليه وسلم قَالَ: لاَ تَجْعَلُوا بُيُوتَكُمْ مَقَابِرَ إِنَّ الشَّيْطَانَ يَنْفِرُ مِنَ الْبَيْتِ الَّذِى تُقْرَأُ فِيهِ سُورَةُ الْبَقَرَةِ [صحيح مسلم]

The Messenger of Allah said: "Do not turn your houses into graveyards. Satan runs away from the house in which Surah *Al-Baqarah* is recited." [Sahih *al-Muslim*]

عَنِ النَّبِيِّ صلى الله عليه وسلم قَالَ: يُقَالُ لِصَاحِبِ الْقُرْآنِ اقْرَأْ وَارْتَقِ وَرَتِّلْ كَمَا كُنْتَ تُرَتِّلُ فِي الدُّنْيَا فَإِنَّ مَنْزِلَكَ عِنْدَ آخِرِ آيَةٍ تَقْرَؤُهَا [سنن أبي داود]

The Messenger of Allah said: "It shall be said – meaning to the one who memorised the Qur'an – 'Recite, and rise up, recite (melodiously) as you would recite in the world. For indeed your rank shall be at the last Ayah you recited." [Sunan *Abi Dawood*]

عَنِ النَّبِيِّ صلى الله عليه وسلم قَالَ: مَنْ قَرَأَ حَرْفًا مِنْ كِتَابِ اللَّهِ فَلَهُ بِهِ حَسَنَةٌ وَالْحَسَنَةُ بِعَشْرِ أَمْثَالِهَا لاَ أَقُولُ الم حَرْفٌ وَلَكِنْ أَلِفٌ حَرْفٌ وَلاَمٌ حَرْفٌ وَمِيمٌ حَرْفٌ [سنن الترمذي]

The Messenger of Allah said: "Whoever recites a letter from the Book of Allah, he will be credited with a good deed, and a good deed gets a ten-fold reward. I do not say that Alif-Lam-Mim is one letter, but Alif is a letter, Lam is a letter and Mim is a letter." [Sunan *Al-Tirmidhi*]

عَنِ النَّبِيِّ صلى الله عليه وسلم قَالَ: إِنَّ لِلَّهِ أَهْلِينَ مِنَ النَّاسِ قَالُوا يَا رَسُولَ اللَّهِ مَنْ هُمْ؟ قَالَ: هُمْ أَهْلُ الْقُرْآنِ أَهْلُ اللَّهِ وَخَاصَّتُهُ [سنن ابن ماجة]

The Messenger of Allah said: "Allah has His own people among mankind. They [the Companions] said: 'O Messenger of Allah, who are they?' He said: 'The people of the Qur'an, the people of Allah and those who are closest to Him." [Sunan *Ibn Majah*]

قَالَ قَتَادَةُ: اعْمُرُوا بِهِ قُلُوبَكُمْ وَاعْمُرُوا بِهِ بُيُوتَكُمْ قَالَ: أُرَاهُ يَعْنِي الْقُرْآنَ [سنن الدارمي]

Qatadah said: "Populate with it [the Qur'an] your heart, populate with it [the Qur'an] your homes." [Sunan *Al-Darmi*]

قَالَ كَعْبٌ: عَلَيْكُمْ بِالْقُرْآنِ فَإِنَّهُ فَهْمُ الْعَقْلِ وَنُورُ الْحِكْمَةِ وَيَنَابِيعُ الْعِلْمِ وَأَحْدَثُ الْكُتُبِ بِالرَّحْمَنِ عَهْدًا [سنن الدارمي]

Ka'ab said: "Hold onto the Qur'an, verily, it sharpens the understanding, it is the light for wisdom, it is the fountain of knowledge and the latest book of the Lord." [Sunan *Al-Darmi*]

# Etiquettes of reading the Qur'an

The Qur'an is the means of guidance, the criterion, the revealed, and the mother of all books, the spiritual guide and the complete way of life. The sanctity of the Qur'an demands it to be treated with honour and reverence.

Some etiquettes of reading the Qur'an are mentioned below:

1) The intention of attachment with the Qur'an should be for the benefits of the hearafter; not gaining the temporary treasures of this world.
2) Making sure the Qur'an is only touched in the state of purity.
3) Whilst in the state of impurity, one should not touch the Qur'an with his sleeves, etc.
4) It is best to avoid touching the translations and commentaries of the Qur'an whilst in the state of impurity.
5) Do not read the Qur'an by memory as well whilst in the state of menstrual bleeding, etc.
6) Recite the Qur'an with regularity.
7) Leave all other occupations when attached with the Qura'nic recitation.
8) Popularise the reciting and message of the Qur'an.
9) Recite the Qur'an both; alone and in groups. Give your family a share of your recitation.
10) Do not read the Qur'an in a place where it could disturb others.
11) Ponder upon the meaning and message of the Qur'an and make yourself a physical manifestation of the Qur'an. Think of how the Prophet and the Companions used to bring the Qur'an into their physical lives.
12) Learn the correct method of pronunciation and recite accordingly.
13) Keep the Qur'an in a respectful place.
14) When reciting the Qur'an sit in a clean place, preferably facing *Qiblah* on two knees.
15) Purify yourself with the recitation; inwardly and outwardly.
16) Begin the recitation with استعاذة and بسملة.
17) Try praying the Qur'an with the best possible voice without trying to imitate any un-Islamic material.
18) Bring emotion within the recitation; repeating verses, asking for blessing whilst reciting the verses of mercy, seeking refuge when reciting the verses of punishment.
19) Realise how fortunate you are whilst reciting, you have been blessed by Allah with the recitation of his speech.

20) Imagine the Qur'an speaking directly to you whilst reciting. Try applying the verse to yourself or relevance to modern time.
21) It is disliked to pray the Qur'an whilst you are tired and sleepy.
22) Read authentic translations of the Qur'an; this will help in creating the correct emotions when reciting.
23) Try memorising as much as possible from the Qur'an.
24) Recite the memorised portion of the Qur'an in the *salaah*.
25) Whenever the verses of *sijdah al-tilawah* appear, perform the *sijdah*.

# Method of memorising the Qur'an

Memorising the Qur'an was from amongst the noble Sunnah of the Prophet *Muhammad* ﷺ, scholars have written a few guidelines which are useful in aiding the memorisation of the Qur'an.

1) Stop all forms of sins.
2) Understand the importance of the Qur'an; understand with full conviction that it is the revelation from Allah (without any changes).
3) Fulfil the etiquettes of the Qur'an to ones best ability.
4) Memorise daily on a regular basis. Even if the memorised portion is little, do it on a regular basis.
5) Read loudly when memorising.
6) Repeat the portion (verse) many times.
7) Many scholars used to memorise the Qur'an by writing it on a paper; writing will also aid in memorising.
8) Listen to the memorised portion from another reciter.
9) Pray the memorised portion to somebody else, (preferably a tutor).
10) Continuously recite the memorised portion within *salaah*.
11) Most importantly, try understanding and then acting upon the Qur'an, thereafter conveying the message to others.
12) Finally, it is very important to continuously make supplications to Almighty Allah that he makes the learning, remembering and acting of the Qur'an easy for oneself.

# Chain of Qur'anic recitation

The authenticity of any subject is based on the validity of the chain of transmitters. Similarly, the authenticity of the Qur'an and Hadeeth is based upon the chain of transmitters. Muhammad bin Sireen mentioned 'Indeed this knowledge is faith, so carefully consider from whom you take your faith'[Sahih Muslim: Introduction: 26]. Fulfilling the obligation of notifying the readers of the chain, I mention, that I learnt the Qur'an in the ten different modes and its recitation rules from my honourable teacher Qari Muhammad Zuber Falahi. The remaining chain is indicated below.

|  |  |  |
|---|---|---|
| 1 | Qari Muhammad Zuber Falahi | القارئ محمّد زبير الفلاحي |
| 2 | Qari Muhammad Siddique Sansrodi Falahi | القارئ محمّد صدّيق سانسرودي الفلاحي |
| 3 | Qari Anees Ahmed Khan | القارئ أنيس أحمد خان |
| 4 | Qari Muhib al-deen Ahmed | القارئ محبّ الدين أحمد |
| 5 | Qari Ziya' al-Din Ahmad Ilahabadi | القارئ ضياء الدين إله آبادي |
| 6 | Qari 'Abd al-Rahman al-Makki | القارئ عبد الرحمن بن محمّد بشير خان المكّي ثمّ إله آبادي الحنفيّ |
| 7 | Shaykh 'Abd al-Allah bin Muhammad Bashir al-Makki | الشيخ عبد الله بن محمّد بشير خان المكّي |
| 8 | Shaykh Ibrahim Sa'ad bin 'Ali | الشيخ إبراهيم سعد بن عليّ |
| 9 | Shaykh Hasan Budayr | الشيخ حسن بدير |
| 10 | Shaykh Muhammad bin Ahmad al-Mutawalli | الشيخ محمّد بن أحمد المتوليّ |
| 11 | Shaykh Ahmad al-Durri al-Tihami | الشيخ السيّد أحمد الدرّي التهامي |
| 12 | Shaykh Ahmad Salmunah | الشيخ أحمد سلمونه |
| 13 | Shaykh Ibrahim al-'Ubaydi | السيّد إبراهيم العبيدي |
| 14 | Shaykh Abdurrahman al-Ujhuri al-Maliki | الشيخ عبد الرحمن الأجهوريّ المالكيّ |
| 15 | Shaykh Ahmad al-Baqari | الشيخ أحمد البقريّ الشهير بأبي السماح |
| 16 | Shaykh Muhammad bin al-Qasim al-Baqari | الشيخ محمّد بن القاسم البقريّ |
| 17 | Shaykh 'Abd al-Rahman al-Yamani | الشيخ عبد الرحمن اليمنيّ |
| 18 | Shaykh Shahhadhah al-Yamani | الشيخ شحاذه اليمنيّ |
| 19 | Shaykh 'Abd al-Haq al-Sunbati | الشيخ أحمد بن عبد الرحمن السنباطيّ |
| 20 | Shaykh Shahhadhah al-Yamani | الشيخ شحاذاه اليمنيّ |
| 21 | Shaykh Nasir al-Din al-Tablawi | الشيخ ناصر الدين الطبلاويّ |
| 22 | Shaykh al-Islam Zakariyya al-Ansari | شيخ الإسلام زكريّا الأنصاريّ |
| 23 | Shaykh Abu N'aim Ridhwan al-'Uqbi | الشيخ أبو نعيم رضوان بن أحمد العقبيّ ومحمّد النويريّ |

| | | |
|---|---|---|
| 24 | Shaykh Muhammad bin al-Jazari | الشيخ محمّد بن الجزريّ |
| 25 | Shaykh Abu Muhammad 'Abd al-Rahman bin Ahmad al-Shafe'e and<br>Shaykh Abu 'Abd al-Allah Muhammad bin 'Abd al-Rahman al-Hanafi | الشيخ أبو محمّد عبد الرحمن بن أحمد الشافعيّ<br>والشيخ أبو عبد الله محمّد بن عبد الرحمن الحنفيّ |
| 26 | Shaykh Abu 'Abd al-Allah bin 'Abd al-Khaliq al-Sa'igh | الشيخ أبو عبد الله محمّد بن عبد الخالق الصائغ |
| 27 | Shaykh Abu al-Hasan 'Ali bin Shuja' | الشيخ أبو الحسن علي بن شجاع |
| 28 | Shaykh Abu al-Qasim bin Firruh al-Shatibi | الشيخ أبو القاسم بن فيّره الشاطبي |
| 29 | Shaykh Abu al-Hasan 'Ali bin Hudhayl | الشيخ أبو الحسن علي بن هذيل |
| 30 | Shaykh Abu Dawood Sulaiman bin Najah | الشيخ أبو داود سليمان بن نجاح |
| 31 | Imam Abu 'Amre 'Uthman bin Sa'eed al-Dani | الإمام أبو عمرو عثمان بن سعيد الداني |
| 32 | Shaykh Abu al-Hasan Tahir bin Ghalbun | الشيخ أبي الحسن طاهر بن غلبون المقرئ |
| 33 | Shaykh Abu al-Hasan 'Ali bin Muhammad bin Salih al-Hashimi | الشيخ أبو الحسن عليّ بن محمّد بن صالح الهاشميّ |
| 34 | Shaykh Abu al-'Abbas Ahmad bin Sahal al-Ushnani | الشيخ أبو العبّاس أحمد بن سهل الأشنانيّ |
| 35 | Shaykh Abu Muhammad 'Ubayd bin Sabbah | الشيخ أبو محمّد عبيد بن صباح |
| 36 | Shaykh Hafs al-Asadi | الشيخ حفص الأسديّ |
| 37 | Shaykh Abu Bakr 'Aasim bin Abi al-Najud al-Kufi | الشيخ أبو بكر عاصم بن أبي النجود الكوفيّ |
| 38 | Zir bin Hubaysh and Abu 'Abd al-Allah bin Habeeb al-Sulami | زرّ بن حبيش الأسديّ وأبو عبد الله بن حبيب السلميّ |
| 39 | Uthman bin Affan, Ali bin Abi Talib, Ubayy bin k'ab, Abd al-Allah bin Mas'ud, Zaid bin Thabit | عثمان بن عفان وعليّ بن أبي طالب وأبيّ بن كعب وعبد الله بن مسعود وزيد بن ثابت |
| 40 | Prophet Muhammad | محمّد بن عبد الله صلّى الله عليه وسلّم |
| 41 | Jibraeel | جبرئيل |
| 42 | Al-Lawh al-Mahfooz (the Preserved tablet) | اللوح المحفوظ |
| 43 | Almighty Allah | ربّ العالمين |

# Other publications
## of Jamiatul Ilm Wal Huda

---

### 1000 Hadith for Memorisation
This book is a compilation of a 1000 authentic narrations from the six famous books, it is designed in chapter form. The book has originally been created for memorisation, yet it can be useful for general reading as well.

---

### Usool al-Hadith (in Arabic)
This book is aimed at teaching Usool al-Hadith to an intermediate level; in an easy format. It is filled with tables and flowcharts; this style has been adopted to make the subject as easy as possible to understand. Furthermore, flowcharts have been added at the end of the book which covers majority of the subject.

---

### Mantiq (in Arabic)
This book is aimed at teaching the classical Mantiq (logic) terms to an intermediate level; in an easy format. It is filled with tables and flowcharts; this style has been adopted to make the subject as easy as possible to understand. Furthermore, flowcharts have been added at the end of the book which covers majority of the subject.

---

### Zahratun Nahw (part 1)
This book is designed for teaching Nahw (Arabic syntax) for the beginner level. It has adopted a very simple style with very simple terms indicated. The depth of the subject has been avoided; aiming to consolidate the very basics of grammar for the learners.

---

### Hidayatun Nahw (with Q&A in English)
The book Hidayatun Nahw is a book taught in many places for intermediate level nahw. However, due to its complex text, many readers find many parts of the text difficult to solve. Therefore, for the english speaking readers, this book was designed with the intention of making the complex text of the book easier for understanding. Hence, the english question & answers do not go into much detail beyond the content of the book; it is more based on solving the book.

---

### Das Sabak (in Urdu & English)
The book Das Sabak is a book taught in many institutes as a beginners guide for Arabic learning. The book covers ten very important topics of Arabic grammer; allowing the students to become equipped with the foundation before enhancing to intermediate level. The book was designed to make translation of the Qur'an easier for beginners; covering most words upto half of the first para. However, as the book was written in Urdu, it became hard for the English speaking audience to take benefit from the book; hence, the need arose to make a parallel English version of the book. The Urdu has been kept within the book, with explanatory English notes for each chapter.